Henry Alexander Wittke

Artificial Intelligence

Henry Alexander Wittke

Artificial Intelligence

An Approach to Assess the Impact on the Information Economy

Tectum Verlag

Henry Alexander Wittke
Artificial Intelligence
An Approach to Assess the Impact on the Information Economy

ISBN 978-3-8288-4459-9
eBook 978-3-8288-7480-0

Umschlaggestaltung: Tectum Verlag, unter Verwendung des Bildes # 587929622 von buffaloboy | www. shutterstock.com

Printed in Germany

Informationen zum Verlagsprogramm finden Sie unter
www.tectum-verlag.de

Bibliografische Informationen der Deutschen Nationalbibliothek
Die Deutsche Nationalbibliothek verzeichnet diese Publikation in der Deutschen Nationalbibliografie; detaillierte bibliografische Angaben sind im Internet über http://dnb.ddb.de abrufbar.

Foreword

The fact that democracies are changing during the process of digitalization is undisputed today. The political handling of these changes will be decisive for the (our) future. Minor challenges arise in those (few) areas in which current trends can simply be extrapolated. However, major political and social challenges arise from "black swans", events that divide the course of time into a "before" and an "after". Artificial intelligence (AI) is both, a minor and a major political challenge: On the one hand, usage of weak AI leads to rapid but anticipatable developments. On the other hand, the development of strong AI is a "black swan", an "event horizon", beyond which serious (political) analysis is impossible.

During his time in Hamburg, Henry Wittke and I have often debated about artificial intelligence. Our discussions at the time - especially on AI's impact on the economy - marked the starting point of a long line of dialogues he had with cutting-edge experts in the US, particularly at Harvard University. The insights and findings are documented in this monograph.

Which impact will AI have on the Information Economy and on society within the next 10-15 years? Will political systems be able to support the beneficial uses of AI while softening the malicious side effects? Henry Wittke addresses these issues in a rigorous and very thoughtful manner. His insights are important for decision makers as well as citizens: During the next five years, he predicts merely a minor transformation of the character of human-machine interaction at work, but not a fundamental change in the structure of the economy. No reason to worry, then? Certainly not, since according to Wittke, things will look different in 15 years' time: widespread use of strong AI will have significantly reduced the number and importance of human-machine tandems at work. More jobs will have been destroyed than new ones created - even in the information sector. This may lead to social upheavals and unrest, unparalleled in the recent history of western democracies.

So, it's high time to talk about the political and social side-effects of AI. This book is a timely and thoughtful offer to start this endeavor.

Gary S. Schaal

Table of Contents

1. Introduction

1.1. Relevance and "Problem Puzzle"

An ongoing and seemingly unstoppable digital transformation brings about new options, opportunities but also challenges to individuals, organizations, companies and societies alike. The everyday gets more and more influenced by drivers like the creation of gigantic amounts of data. Now the total amount of data being produced doubles every year. In 2016 the world produced as much data as in the entire history of humankind through 2015. It is estimated, that in ten years, the available amount of data will double every twelve hours (cf. Helbing et al. 2017: 2). In the wake of exponentially rising data, also the field of Artificial Intelligence (AI), is developing significantly. The increasing availability of a vast amount of data is therefore helping the growth and applications of so-called AI. Recent breakthroughs in the field of neural networks and deep learning algorithms as a part of machine learning, increase AI's potential to disrupt the world's largest industries. For example, in the business sector, AI is poised to have a transformational impact. Although it is already in use in most companies around the globe, most big opportunities for AI deployment have not yet been tapped. Current developments in the field of AI alarm governments, seeing the potential consequences on the workforce and thus societal change while also being seemingly helpless against uncontrollable and powerful digital players such as Google or Facebook. They are increasingly penetrating the so-called real economic sectors, also using more and more AI-applications and transforming the rules and fabric how actors engage in socio-economic relationships.

From a scientific perspective, there are different perceptions of AI, which will be categorized and also simplified within this thesis into weak and strong AI. It is assumed that weak AI-driven automation is already transforming the way in which societies and economies are organized. But the impact and transformation caused by the beginning of strong AI and its deep learning algorithms could be much more profound than changes origination from weak AI. As with any profound change, there will be players winning from this transformation but also losers. Vast transformation processes are not new. But the difference this time under strong AI is that most observers feel that job losses in established sectors will occur at an unpreceded level, while only relatively few new jobs will be suitable or created for the same work staff at all. It is further being argued that another difference to previous technical transformation is as follows: Technological advancement destroys low-skilled jobs. Higher education would secure new jobs in different sectors. However, this time, it could not be the case. Even the highest skilled employees could end up with machines and systems doing their work. Instead of „transformation", i.e. a switch from resources from one sector to the other, there will just be: idle human resources, further caused by a huge skill gap. And this on a massive scale. An imaginable scenario like this caused by strong AI will strongly influence the so-called information society, basic principles of capitalism and the foundations of today's societies.

However, looking at the current research, a consensus or clear-cut definition what might constitute AI precisely as a base for such a conceptual framework is missing. Further, only a little research has been conducted; understandingly given the relatively recent occurrence of digitalization using AI and the few available results vary strongly. On the one hand, differentiation between strong and weak AI are done weakly or not at all, using general perceptions of Computerization or Digitalization. On the other hand, warnings on the effects of strong AI are being often made without intending to provide detailed insights into the precise effects. Possibly, only once we have understood and developed a concept of AI separating AI from other digitalization trends can we estimate the impact of AI on workplaces, economies, and societies and provide recommendations to cope (or not to cope) with the effects of AI. Concerning the technology assessment of AI and the aforementioned technological upheavals, the identified research gap seems to be essential to be filled.

The main problem with AI is the lack of measurability of change. Based on the literature and the complexity of AI itself, it can be seen that there are no quantitative measuring methods, instruments or indices for both the current state of the art and the possible uses of strong AI.

> "Without the relevant data for reasoning about the state of AI technology, we are essentially "flying blind" in our conversations and decision-making related to AI." (AI100 2017: 54).

This research gap has to be closed in the future. The need has already been identified, but against the background of the exponential character of AI, other Big Data-based technologies are often described as increas-

ing complexity research and a major challenge in the wake of the digital revolution (cf. Rouhiainen 2018; Gershenfeld et al. 2017).
However, several approaches established so far merely base on comparing AI with human intelligence. Others are comparing technological milestones over time, the rise of financial expenditures within the AI sector, ongoing research projects or related parameters to assess the current state of the art. There is a lack of standardized methods for example to distinguish different neural networks or deep learning algorithms based on exact scales, growth rates in terms of the speed of developments of the technical field as itself to track the societal transformation. Pioneering projects that address this research gap include, for example, the scientists working on the AI Index at Stanford University with other research facilities. Only if the current state of the art is better analyzed, and methods developed for that investigation this problem puzzle might be solved and future impact of AI better assessed.
Overall, we recognize that no consideration of the past helps to solve the real challenge and there is not enough suitable state of research. Therefore, the following theoretical approach should be proposed.

1.2. Theoretical Approach

This thesis seeks to investigate, which effects in particular strong AI could have on our today's societies. For this undertaking, a conceptual framework is required.

As Steven Hawkings said:

> "The rise of powerful AI will be either the best or the worst thing ever to happen to humanity. We do not yet know which." (Ingham 2018)

To seek to investigate if AI might be the best or worst thing to happen, this thesis attempts to provide a basic framework using concepts of strong and weak AI and thus to make a small contribution to the initial research available today.
The concept of the Information Economy as the economic dimension of the information society shall form the generic base of the methodological approach. The Information Economy concept is widely acknowledged as a way to describe highly developed large economies. Further, it can be adjusted to the purpose of this investigation and enriched by the notion of strong AI.

To then attempt to estimate the impact of AI on economies, we use Machlup's segmentation of economies in the information society age: Education, Information Services, Information Machines, The Media of Communication, Research and Development. These five segments shall be used as research objects to discuss the impact strong AI might have on them beyond weak AI or common digitization trends.

Special notion is placed on employment and labor skills since – without taking the argument too far already here – it is assumed that highly developed labor skills are a necessary precondition for employment in AI impacted segments of the economy. But also not a guarantee. Often it is argued that AI will eliminate jobs (cf. Brougham/ Haar 2017). From here follows the next reason to emphasize the effects on labor and employment. If it can be argued in the case studies that all of Machlup's five economic segments could be strongly affected by AI in terms of job losses, then an entire economy might face substantial rises in unemployment. If so, a seemingly segmental transformation issue on a rather micro-economic level might turn into vast macro-economic and thus potentially political problem.
Thus, based on the results of the case studies, this thesis will switch to a more macro-level approach. Which economic and political impacts could entire societies face if the effects of AI are profound and widespread? What will be the effect on work and labor as a value system for individuals and societies?

In this second analysis following the analysis on Machlup's economic segments, different questions shall be raised and different scenarios shall be discussed:
For example, what happens in case of rising mass unemployment or social inequality? Such a development could involve social instability, lost identity, profound disillusionment with "the political and economic system" or even riots. Could the entire notion of capitalism be questioned in the wake of strong AI? Which responses might politics and societies as a whole develop? Which social solutions or strategies on a large-scale are needed for upcoming social challenges?
We will look at two possible options: On the one hand, a basic income as an approach to alleviate the effects of unemployment on individuals but also as a new way labor and income distribution could be organized: The allocation of a secure income to unemployed persons and thus the acceptance that parts of the labor force receive income from working while

others are free to pursue ends and goals with a basic income without working in traditional contractual employment schemes.
On the other hand, we will look at skill development, at the so-called information worker and show how strong AI will change the employment in the information society and what skills are important for a workforce in the age of AI. Retraining and educating this workforce seems to be very important, and the human-machine symbiosis could be essential. It will discuss how people can work together in an optimal relationship with robots and AI-driven applications. Tasks getting done by machines and others by people could be even smarter than either side of the equation.
Based on these discussions, the thesis then attempts to draw conclusions and first initial recommendations to policy makers. There might be many complex and intertwined ones, not feasible to handle in this thesis. All in all this upcoming paper will contribute to this goal by discussing political possibilities of actions in the final part of the research.

1.3. Structure of the Thesis

In the light of the above-described research approach, this thesis is structured as follows: The second chapter will concentrate on AI. Here, a differentiation of AI into weak and strong AI will be introduced. Then it will look at the current state of deployment of AI. It will be discussed that economic actors actively and strongly already pursue the introduction of AI, seeking efficiency gains and higher profit margins. The following third chapter will develop the concept of the information economy as the economic dimension of the information society. Also, the evolution of Information and Communication Technology (ICT) and the change of work, as well as the information worker, will be described. In the last part of the chapter, AI will be transferred into the context of the information society, and the hypotheses for the analysis of this research should be made. This is followed by the development of hypotheses to start to produce an assessment of the impact of AI on economic activity in information societies.
In chapter fifth, the hypotheses will be applied to Machlup's information society framework. Here, this thesis looks at the industry sectors defined by Machlup. It will be argued, that almost all sectors will likely be deeply affected by AI. While chapter fifth takes a rather "micro" view on industry segments, chapter six again will develop further hypotheses, arguing that actions are required to alleviate the effects of AI. In chapter seven the analysis will change to a rather macro-political view. If many

economic sectors are affected, what implications may arise for the entire information society and for the political sphere? Before discussing options for such actions, chapter seven will seek to further establish the validity of the action claim put forward by looking at already occurring impacts of AI. These short elaborations seek to foster the rather theoretical argument to Machlup's framework with current evidence. Then, chapter eight discusses areas for actions to be taken, here proposing the need for further education for so-called knowledge workers, retraining the workforce of the future or a basic income. Finally, chapter nine will do a short critical review of the research so far, and then the conclusion will finish this thesis.

2. Artificial Intelligence

The beginning of the following chapter will concentrate on creating a definition of artificial intelligence and describes briefly what makes this emerging technology so powerful. Nowadays artificial intelligence is regularly used by people as shorthand to talk about everything from building robotic process automation tools, to chatbots, neural networks or deep learning (cf. Donovan 2017). The reappearing boom of AI in recent years in all things artificial intelligence catalyzed by breakthroughs in the area of machine learning. Machine learning can be defined as a set of methods that can automatically detect patterns in data, and then use the uncovered patterns to predict future data, or to perform other kinds of decision making under uncertainty. It involves training computers to perform tasks based on examples, rather than by relying on programming by a human. In short, it is a self-teaching computer system (cf. Murphy 2012: 32; Piovesan/ Ntiri 2018: 1f.; Wired 2018; Fraser 2017).

The most relevant types of machine learning are supervised, unsupervised and reinforcement learning. The details of each of these methods are beyond the scope of this paper. Today these methods can be combined with a deep learning architecture, which makes machine learning approaches ways more powerful. Deep learning operates by using artificial neural networks. They contain layers of nodes that in some ways mimic the neurons in the human brain, to train computer systems on large quantities of data to recognize patterns in digital representations of sounds, images, and other data. Every single layer of neurons takes the data from the layer below it, performs a calculation, and provides its

output to the layer above it. This architecture can be combined with an unsupervised process to learn the features of the underlying data, such as the edge of the face, and then provide that information to supervised learning algorithms to recognize features as well as the final result, which in the example of a photo of a human face correctly identifies a person in the picture (visual recognition). Besides these combinations, the most promising method is reinforcement learning combined with deep learning, so-called deep reinforcement learning systems (cf. Buchanan et al. 2017: 6ff., Murphy 2012: 32; Piovesan/ Ntiri 2018: 1f.). This combination is a powerful set of techniques used to generate control and action systems whereby autonomous agents are trained to take actions given an environment state to maximize future rewards. Though nascent, recent advances within this area are impressive. In addition to its recent victories in the game of Go, the software company Google DeepMind has achieved superhuman performance in several Atari games (cf. Fortunato et al. 2017). These short mentioned successful use-cases are notable technological milestones. Amongst other use-cases they have the ability to change the economic landscape, creating new opportunities for business value creation and cost reduction (cf. Esteva et al. 2017; Brynjolfsson et al. 2017: 3).
Intending to the potential of AI, in combination with recent improvements in big data, cloud or connected devices and the support of possible future technologies, such as quantum computers, this paradigm shift could be further stimulated. By that it is important to realize that the early leading adaptors of these emerging technological possibilities in the field of AI also take responsibility for their actions, even to make sure that everybody has a common idea what AI means exactly for individuals, organizations, companies, and societies.

The following chapter is intended to define artificial intelligence with the help of the definition of intelligence. After that, a differentiation of AI into weak and strong AI will be introduced. Then, a definition of AI for the following research should be made. The last part of this chapter will look at the current state of deployment of AI. It will be discussed that economic actors actively and strongly already pursue the introduction of AI, seeking efficiency gains and higher profit margins.

2.1. Intelligence and Artificial Intelligence

Starting with a definition attempt of artificial intelligence, it helps to differentiate AI from the basic concept of intelligence. So far, there are several different types of definitions, because intelligence exists at different levels and there is no consensus on how to distinguish them precisely. However, similarities can be detected under different definition attempts. In essence, it describes a general mental ability that includes the ability to discern rules and reasons, think abstractly, learn from experience, develop complex ideas, plan and solve problems. Artificial intelligence, in turn, is supposed to reproduce the aspects as mentioned earlier of human behavior to be able to act humanly in this way, without being part of a sentient organism. Thus it is intelligence that is artificially made. It includes qualities and abilities such as solving problems, explaining, learning, understanding speech as well as the flexible reactions of a human being (cf. Gentsch 2018: 17; Marwala/ Hurwitz 2017: 9). Since the middle of the 20th century, AI forms a field within computer science. The aim is to find methods by which human abilities such as the conclusion of experts, mathematical proofing, the recognition of images, the understanding of the natural language or the targeted optimization in any environment can be simulated on computers. These systems should be adaptive — for example, they could query an unknown fact to the user and to save the gained information for reuse. The stored programs and data can be represented in the form of rules (cf. Wedde et al. 1990: 280).

Since it is not possible to find the only one universal definition of Artificial Intelligence, the following definition by Elaine Rich seems to be the most appropriate for this research contribution:

> "Artificial Intelligence is the study of how to make computers do things at which, at the moment, people are better." (Ertel 2016: 2).

It briefly characterizes what scientists have been doing in the field of AI for the last fifty years and what they will do in the future. Humans are still more capable and suitable in most of the fields, but computers and algorithms already offer enormous advantages. Their ability being to dominate more fields in the existing society will increase. Further abilities of AI could evolve exponentially (cf. De Waele 2016: 1). Other scientists say that AI is more like a theory and development of computer systems able to perform tasks usually requiring human intelligence. Alternatively, AI is an activity devoted to making machines intelligent, and intelligence is that quality that enables an entity to function appropriately and with foresight in its environment.

2.2. Different Types of AI

Overall, AI is a sophisticated technology with an equally complex conceptional understanding. There is no universal definition of the term itself. In part, determining what AI is, it is only possible in its context. From a technical point of view, the types of AI are also enormously controversial and cannot be differentiated at first glance. For this purpose, the specific artificial intelligence must be closely examined and tested for their abilities.
So far, extensive tests focus on comparing human intelligence with artificial intelligence using, for example, Alan Turing's so-called Turning Test, widely used since 1950. He tests a machine's ability to exhibit intelligent behavior equivalent to, or indistinguishable from, that of a human (cf. Puget 2017).
An established AI Index or different types of distinguishing levels of AI itself is underrepresented. There are no clear procedures that could differentiate several AI algorithms with the help of specific scalability.

In order not to place the previously outlined technical complexity of today's AI systems in the focus of this chapter, the various differentiation and types of AI will be fundamentally differentiated into two types for this work: Weak and strong AI.

2.2.1. Weak AI vs. Strong AI

Weak AI or rather narrow AI describes an interpretation of AI according to which conscious awareness is a property of specific brain processes and whereas any physical behavior can, in principle at least, be simulated by a computer using purely computational procedures; computational simulation cannot in itself evoke conscious awareness (cf. Colman 2015). According to this view, the weak artificial intelligence is usually entrusted with concrete application problems, which do not depend on logical thinking, decision making or even not based on consciousness. It primarily serves humans as an information provider on which it bases their decisions. These include, for example, the following areas of responsibility: Expert systems, navigation systems, voice recognition or the automatic correction suggestions for digital search functions (cf. van der Touw 2016). Some common examples of weak AI are in consumer applications such as Apples Siri or Google Maps. It is combining several narrow AI techniques plus access to extensive data in a cloud (cf.

Greenwald 2011). In shorthand, weak AI can be described as: „devices and applications that do specialist tasks much better than we ourselves could do them, mostly because they number-crunch in ways we can't.“ (Souter 2018: 1). However, it is still supervised programming, which means there is a programmed output or action for given inputs. So weak AI might behave like a robot or manufacturing line is thinking on its own.

Compared with that, Strong AI or Artificial General Intelligence (AGI) is a more complex approach that might change output based on given goals and input data.

> "An interpretation of artificial intelligence according to which all thinking is computation, from which it follows that conscious thought can be explained in terms of computational principles, and that feelings of conscious awareness are evoked merely by certain computations carried out by the brain or (in principles at least) by a computer." (Colman 2015b).

So a program could do something that it was not programmed to do when it detects a pattern and determines a more efficient way to reaching the goal it was given (cf. Kerns 2017: 2). The strong AI wants to create the most powerful computer systems imaginable. However, the utmost efficiency imaginable is the reproduction of human intelligence. In this way, strong AI can be described as the highest level of sapience or as machines with human-like intelligence and beyond (cf. Sarkar 2018: 1; Alpcan 2017: 2). „Strong“ is not this output of strong AI, what it already has created, which is in their own perspective rather "weak", but what it promises to deliver (Sesink 2012: 3f.). Regardless of this, one often speaks of strong artificial intelligence as when a machine has the same intellectual abilities as a human or even surpasses it. A perception like this would also mean that no longer only people are competing for a particular job with each other, but also the with strong AI itself as if it were a human worker.

Current examples for the early beginning of strong AI could be seen in deep reinforcement systems playing chess or go, soar cognitive architecture, autonomous vehicles or AI systems like Google Duplex. However, strong AI has not achieved his potential yet. Based on AI and its often quoted exponential character it can be assumed that strong AI might be relevant in the near future. However, it is still controversially discussed. While some argue the opposite that the full potential of strong AI will be a long-term achievement, others argue that it will never be reached.

Based on a few studies, some scholars predict that computers will reach human intelligence around 2029, because AI is an exponentially increasing technology and undergoing a massive acceleration driven by an immense growth especially in available data and the rapid evolution of algorithms. The full potential of strong AI, so-called real singularity or superintelligence of machines when they are more intelligent than humans at all, will come by 2045 (cf. Makridakis 2017: 11f; Kurzweil 2005). Furthermore, other scholars asked 60 experts of an Artificial General Intelligence Conference (2011) to answer the question, if they believe that AGI will be effectively implemented in the following timeframe. Of the experts surveyed, 43.3 percent estimated that it would be before the year 2030, 25 percent estimated between 2030 and 2049, 20 percent said between 2050 and 2099, 20 percent said after 2100, and 1.7 percent said never. In result, more than two-thirds of respondents predicted that AGI would occur before 2050. A more recent survey conducted in 2016 by Etzioni et al. was related to superintelligence, as an often mentioned ability of strong AI. Etzioni's question was based on Nick Bostroms book, which defined superintelligence as an intellect that is much smarter than the best human brains in practically every field, including scientific creativity, general wisdom, and social skills. Etzioni asked the experts when they think superintelligence could be a reality. The answers of the 80 responders are summarized as follows: Nobody thought in the next ten years, 7.5 percent estimated between the next ten and 25 years, 67.5 percent in more than 25 years, 25.0 percent decided to say never. These results put the start of superintelligence later than that of Kurzweil survey but still a realistic scenario (cf. Makridakis 2017: 11f.).

To return the perspective of this work and a possible qualitative investigation of strong AI, all in all, there are five areas that are often associated with strong AI: Awareness, self-perception, sensibility, wisdom, and feelings. However, it is still unclear to what extent these capabilities are interrelated. For example, if awareness is necessary to think logically (cf. van der Touw 2016).

Based on these basic descriptions strong AI should be seen in the course of this research with the following characteristics: Logical thinking, natural language, self-learning, self-structured planning and decision-making in uncertainty.

In conclusion, there are significant differences between the two types of AI. The term Strong AI refers to the type of AI that has specific capabilities similar to those of human intelligence. This concept differs significantly from the existing computing systems and mainstream AI algorithms, already described as weak AI. Weak AI-based systems are successful in solving specific problems when the problem context is provided directly by a human programmer. In contrast, strong AI is much deeper and broader in its ambition as it aims for human-like flexibility, understanding, and creativity (cf. Alpcan 2017: 1f.).

2.2.2. AI Definition for the Analysis

The following part of this research will focus on the early form of strong AI. Although strong AI is not being used today as predicted by its potential, some scholars expect that the necessary technical developments will evolve rapidly in the next years. By looking into empiricism, tendencies and the early beginning of strong AI could already be identified. Examples are deep reinforcement learning systems winning in chess or go against the human world champions, AI systems like Google Duplex or autonomous vehicles. Nevertheless, against the background of the critical literature as well as the current technical limitations of strong AI, a weak form of strong AI should be used for the analysis of this research. The core of this definition will thus be formed concerning the previous chapters and by its current state of the art. So the basic understanding of strong AI for the following analysis within this research will be described as follows:

In general, build on weak AI because it is still working in the economy. But the AI system has also be described at least with one of the following characteristics of strong AI: Logical thinking, natural language, self-learning, self-structured planning and decision-making in uncertainty. Thus, the definition would theoretically be located between weak and strong AI, but by describing it with one of the mentioned characteristics should mean the system is already an early stage of strong AI. The more of the mentioned characteristics would be fulfilled the more advanced would the strong AI become.
For example, deep reinforcement learning systems winning in chess or go against the human world champions, because of such increasing successes, at least the self-learning characteristic would be evaluated as realistic. Looking at systems like Google Duplex, the natural language

characteristic could be considered as given. In the case of autonomous vehicles, however, several properties of strong AI could already be considered. Both self-learning, self-structured planning and decision-making in uncertainty would be conceivable. Thus, autonomous vehicles would undoubtedly be a showcase example of strong AI within the mobility sector. Based on these examples, it can also be argued that they already go well beyond the complexity measure of weak AI and can, therefore, be seen as the early form of strong AI.

2.3. Place Value of AI in the Economy

Andrew Ng, Professor of Stanford University, coined the phrase that AI seems to be the new electricity. From his perspective, AI will revolutionize all industries of the economy in a similar way to the electrification process of the world (cf. Tomer 2017; AI100 2017: 54). This metaphor is symbolic of current developments and potentials in the field of AI. Artificial Intelligence is undergoing a massive acceleration driven by an immense growth especially in available data and the rapid evolution of algorithms.

The following chart shows most of the different industry sectors. It measures, on the one hand, the current AI adoption, and on the other hand, the future AI demand trajectory:

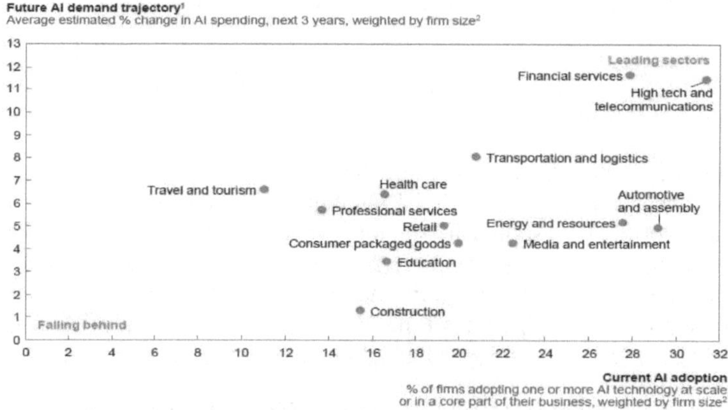

Figure I: Sectors leading in AI adoption today also intend to grow their investment the most. Source: McKinsey 2017:19.

Financial services, high tech and telecommunications are the leading early adopters of Artificial Intelligence and will be the leading industries that adopt AI in the next two years. In addition to this chart, it is also noteworthy that financial services[1] and healthcare[2] seeing the highest increase in their profit margins as a result of AI adoption (cf. Forbes 2017). Within ten years AI and robotics are expected to create an estimated annual so-called creative disruption impact of up to 33 trillion dollars globally. It includes eight trillion to nine trillion of cost reductions across manufacturing and healthcare, nine trillion in cuts to employment costs due to AI-enabled automation of knowledge work and 1.9 trillion in efficiency gains via autonomous cars and drones (cf. Medium 2017). It is predicted that AI may power the next generation of efficiency tools (cf. Motte 2017).

The leading technology firms are in a race to build the best AI and capture a massive market. Thus IBM is working on its Watson, Amazon is banking on Alexa, Apple has Siri. At the same time Google, Facebook, and Microsoft are devoting their research labs to AI and robotics. All of these companies show their public attitude and are highlighting their enthusiasm for Artificial Intelligence (cf. Kelnar 2016; Bajpai 2017; The Guardian 2017; Maney 2016: 1). At the same time, investments in the field of AI are rising considerably. For example tech giants including Baidu and Google spent between 20 billion to 30 billion dollars on Artificial Intelligence in 2016 alone. It includes 90 percent on R&D and deployment, ten percent on Artificial Intelligence acquisitions (cf. Data Collective 2017; Medium 2017; Forbes 2017).

> "The last 10 years have been about building a world that is mobile-first. (…) In the next 10 years, we will shift to a world that is AI-first." (Rieber 2017: 13).

Practitioners place a high expected future value on Artificial Intelligence. The current age of Artificial Intelligence has the potential to disrupt the world's largest industries and is expected to contribute 15,7 trillion us dollar to the global economy by 2030. That is one reason why AI is often called a new wave of innovation or the world's next industrial revolution (cf. Hindu Business Line 2017; Piovesan/ Ntiri 2018; Baron 2016: 1). AI and the widespread adoption of cognitive systems across a

---

[1] AI and advances in robotics will likely disrupt millions of workers within these sectors globally, generating up to 50 percent in productivity gains.

[2] AI-based services will play a growing role in automated support, diagnosis, and advice in healthcare (cf. Medium 2017).

broad range of industries will drive worldwide revenues from nearly 8 billion dollars in 2016 to more than 47 billion dollars in 2020 with banking named as one of the top two industries to lead the charge (cf. IDC 2016). This estimate and assumption based on several parallel developments, which will not be discussed in detail in this research. However, to name a few, the following illustration helps.

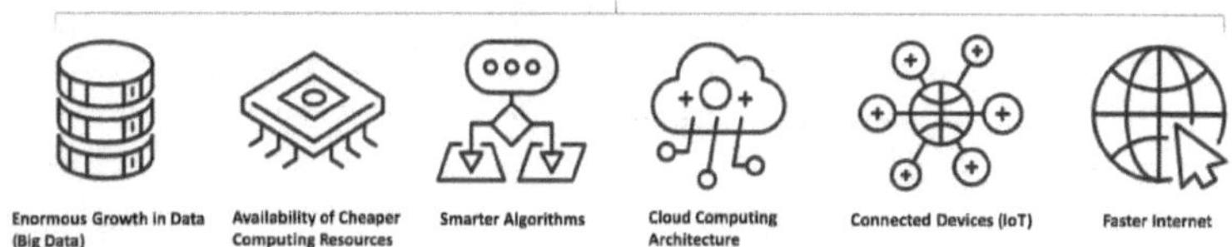

Figure II: Infrastructure Development. Source: Own graphic.

These technological achievements, increasingly powerful hardware, evolving machine learning approaches, and vast new data sets are fueling a transformation of these major global industries such as financial services, healthcare, retail, education, manufacturing and supply chain, mobility or the security sector (cf. Data Collective 2017; Medium 2017).

All in all, the potential of AI in the business sector can be seen in the increase in profit margin and productivity.
Furthermore, AI is seen as a productivity-enhancing factor. A Bank of America Merrill Lynch report predicted that adoption of robots and AI could boost productivity by 30 percent in many industries while cutting manufacturing costs by 18 to 33 percent (cf. Medium 2017). By that, the McKinsey found out:

> "companies who benefit from senior management support for AI initiatives have invested in infrastructure to support its scale and have clear business goals achieve 3 to 15 percentage point higher profit margin." (Forbes 2017).

In addition, the following figure shows the economic impact of artificial AI in developed countries that currently make up almost 50 percent of global gross domestic product (cf. Accenture 2016). More precisely it estimates the increase in labor productivity with AI, more precisely the percentage difference between a baseline without AI improvements and an AI steady state in 2035:

Country	Percentage Increase in Labor Productivity with AI
Sweden	+ 37%
Finland	+ 36%
USA	+ 35%
Japan	+ 34%
Austria	+ 30%
Germany	+ 29%
Netherlands	+ 27%
UK	+ 25%
France	+ 20%

Figure III: Projected Increase in Labor Productivity with AI. Source: Own graphic.

This comparative country illustration, based on analysis by Accenture and Frontier Economics, underlines that AI can be seen as a robust productivity-enhancing factor (cf. Medium 2017). With much of today's businesses making use of AI for the task of increasing their productivity, even a new job title of a "Chief AI Officer" has been introduced to manage the use of AI in the most efficient way (cf. Forbes 2017b; Schrage 2017: 1). In this context, it underlines the importance of using AI as a productivity-enhancing technology with optimal impacts in each company.

In the healthcare sector, an architecture using deep neural networks was tested against 21 board-certified dermatologists and matched their performance in diagnosing skin cancer (cf. Esteva et al. 2017). In the software sector, the social networking company Facebook uses their neural networks for more than 4.5 billion translations every day. For example, image recognition is one reason amongst others, why an increasing number of companies have responded to these opportunities (cf. Brynjolfsson et al. 2017: 3). Another common use-cases are natural language processing, which refers to a system's ability to process and understand human language to convert it into full representations. It holds enormous benefits as well and is for example used in chatbots, real-time text translation or new systems like google duplex (cf. Murphy 2012: 32; Piovesan/ Ntiri 2018: 1f.).

In conclusion, it can be assumed that AI has a revolutionizing impact. However, the whole development of AI in the economy and this desired increase in productivity and profit margin of the companies has far-reaching consequences, which will be analyzed in a later part of this research.

3. Information Society

The information society is a highly abstract and diverse discussed concept of modern industrialized countries, which meaning and development have been described very differently in the past. There is a consensus in the literature that the concept of modern information societies is due to massive societal changes from the second half of the 20th century until modern days, but no consensus when exactly individual countries entered this age of society. The term is also referred to knowledge society, post-industrial society, network society or information age. Depending on the focus of the research and the interests involved, various characteristics are identified and presented for the information society. In general, the term information society can be characterized as important social developments linked to the use of information as well as information and communication technology. Based on a few definitions which seem suitable for the purpose of this research, information society is described as a form of economy and society in which the extraction, storage, processing, communication, dissemination and use of information and knowledge, including growing technical possibilities of interactive communication, plays a crucial role (cf. Kamps 1999: 245; Beniger 1986: 4ff.; Webster 2014; Martin 2005: 4f.)

However, based on the fact that the typology of the information society is so different, the following illustration will cover different approaches:

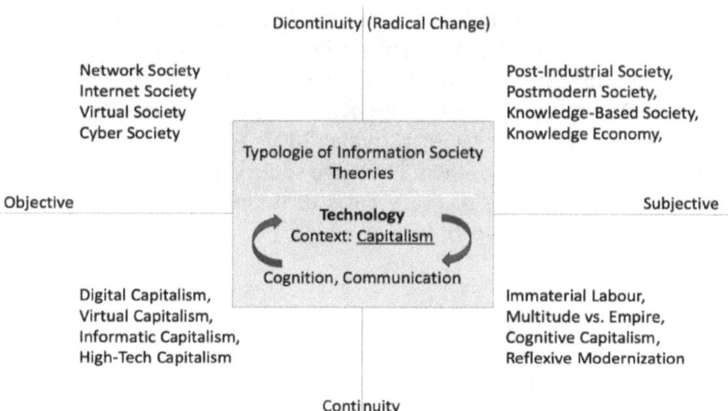

Figure IV: Typology of Information Society Theories. Source: Own graphic, similar: Fuchs 2012: 415.

Shown by this illustration the information society theory discourse can then be theoretically categorized by making use of two axes. The vertical axis distinguishes aspects of societal change, the horizontal axis the informational qualities of these changes (cf. Fuchs 2012: 414f.).

3.1. The Birth of a Concept

From today's scientific perspective, the most relevant ideas of the information society were already formulated from 1960 to 1980 and elaborated within the framework of concepts of knowledge and post-industrial society. At the heart of these concepts lay the analysis of the influence which the increasing role of information and information technologies exerted on the social and economic changes within the societies of that time of Western Europe, USA and Canada or Japan (cf. Kasperkiewicz 2004: 309). Essential theoretical foundations for the information society put the American economist Peter F. Drucker in its work 1969 under the designation knowledge society, based on a previous book from 1962 of Fritz Machlup „The Production and Distribution of Knowledge in the United States“. Machlup described the beginning of a so-called information economy and most people agree that he started it all, although he used the term knowledge industry and not information society. However, he showed that the production of knowledge is an economic activity and is describable with the terms used in the analysis of the industrial sector. In addition to Machlup, Drucker coined the term of the so-called knowledge worker in 1967. He predicted the emergence of a knowledge-based society based on a major increase in the average level of education. As a result of educational expansion in the US, knowledge became a key factor in production, and the knowledge worker the most important figure in the American workforce (cf. Klotz 2009: 4; Duff 1996: 118; Reinecke 2010: 4; Drucker 1969; Karvalic 2007: 6). Later, in his book 1969, he based the concept of the knowledge society on the central thesis that knowledge has become the very basis of the modern economy and society or the real principle of social action (cf. Drucker 1969: 326, Engelhardt 2010: 22).

However, information society was not only the subject of economics or information systems but also of sociology. Daniel Bell, American sociologist and professor of Harvard University from 1970 to 1990, coined the term of the post-industrial society since 1958 and is recognized to be the foremost writer on the information society. It is argued that Bells position has always contained three distinct elements (cf. Klotz 2009: 4; Duff 1998: 373; Webster 2006).

> "One relating to the post-industrial information workforce, a second dealing with information flows (particularly scientific knowledge), and a third concerning computers and the information revolution. Bell's information society thesis is best understood as a synthesis of these elements." (Duff 1998: 373).

He explains this in „The Coming Post-Industrial Society" from 1976, which can be considered paradigmatic for the idea of a profound structural change in industrial society (cf. Bell 1976; Steinbiecker 2011: 50).

In regard to the birth of the exact expression of information society, the concept is also linked to the Japanese terms „Joho Shakai" and „Johoka Shakai". Joho shakai is usually translated into English as the information society but has also been rendered as an information-oriented society, information-conscious society and information-centered society. Johoka Shakai has a sense analogous to industrialized society but is also translated sometimes merely information society. Against this backdrop, the term first emerged in Japanese social sciences in the early 1960's. The first English language reference dates are from 1970 and have to be linked to Yoneji Masuda, who used the expression in his lecture at a conference and appeared in print in the same year. Moreover, in 1971 a systematizing dictionary on information society was published from Johoka Shakai Jiten and many Japanese publications followed (cf. Karvalics 2007: 5f; Duff 1996: 118f.).

> „the realization of a society that brings about a general flourishing state of human intellectual creativity, instead of affluent material consumption" (Masuda 1980: 3).

Masuda interpreted information society as a positive development for humanity, although many new challenges are imminent. More recently but also relevant for the concept of the information society is the sociologist Manuel Castells, the renown sociologist of Berkeley University and author of the groundbreaking book of the so-called Information Age. He claims by long-standing research in more than thirty countries of the world that a new kind of society comes into being - the so-called network society. Castells presented 1996 to 1998 three research publications on this Information Age. First „The Rise of the Network Society", second „The Power of Identity" and third „The End of the Millennium".

His extensive research has been in the wake of capitalist restructuring and based on the revolution in information and communication technologies (cf. Castells 1996: 28ff.). In contrast to Drucker's post-capitalist society and Beil's post-industrial society, Castells speaks of a rejuvenated, informal capitalism based on informationalism, a new mode of development (cf. Castells 1996: 77; Steinbiecker 2011: 79f; Kasperkiewicz 2004: 310).

3.2. Basic Characteristics

Fundamental to the concept of an information society for this research is the social development from an industrial society to a service society based on knowledge in the second half of the 20th century as well as the increase of information processing activities. Information was henceforth described as a distinguishing feature of the modern world. Thus we were entered in an information age, an e-society and stepped into an economy driven by information. For example, British sociologist Frank Webster distinguished five definitions with characteristics of an information society, each of which presents criteria for identifying the new. First technological innovation, second occupational change, third economic value, fourth information flows and fifth the expansion of symbols and signs. The theoretical criterion that he used to classify information society theories is the dimension of society that they primarily focus on. These need not be mutually exclusive, though researcher emphasizes one or other factors in presenting their particular scenarios. However, what these definitions share is the conviction that quantitative changes in information are bringing into being a qualitatively new sort of social system so-called information society. So each definition reasons in much the same way: there is much more information nowadays; therefore information society exists. Webster mentioned as we shall see, there are severe difficulties with this ex-post facto reasoning that argues a cause from a conclusion (cf. Webster 2014: 10f.; Webster 2006: 2, Fuchs 2012: 414).

By taking a closer look at all the different authors and their concepts of information society summarized in the last chapter, there are some common characteristics. Based on these theories, especially on the publications of Drucker, Bell, and Castells, information societies can be described as follows. By that six fundamental dimensions can be considered as the formal framework of an information society:
First were identified new productive forces and new principles of value creation where knowledge, innovation, and technical development - as

opposed to labor, machinery, capital, energy or land - play a crucial role. The new productive forces should demarcate the information society qualitatively from the industrial society. Second, new information and communication technologies are the guiding technology and the epitome of structural change (cf. Steinbicker 2011: 9; Berthoud 2003: 388; May 2000: 3ff.). Moreover, they are paradigmatic for the new knowledge-based industries and play an important role in the transformation of the division of labor, organization, and administration. Third, an organizational change, as the information society goes away from the hierarchical bureaucracy, which was regarded as the organizational model of industrial society. Therefore, new forms and problems of the division of labor of knowledge workers are discussed. Fourth, the structural change of work. Manual activities evolve into high information or knowledge-based activities. Thus, there was an increase in occupations with higher education requirements, which is why from a political perspective, this structural change is assigned central importance. The group of so-called knowledge workers occupies a strategic position in the information society and can be seen as the winner of the transformation process. Important quantitative indicators are thus the growth of the service or information sector in the economy together with the change of occupational structure, which is reflected in the increasing importance of administrative, professional and technical occupations. Fifth, the shifts in the stratification system. Within the information society, education should play the decisive role. Bell even talks about an upcoming meritocracy. Sixth the power structures such as the role of the state and the relationship between the state and the economy changed fundamentally in comparison to the previous industrial societies (cf. Steinbicker 2011: 9f., Machlup 1962: 48, Bell 1976).

Overall, the emergence of the concept of the information society was part of the mentioned technological revolution and significant social changes. The central characteristics of the new social formation include not only information but also service and knowledge (cf. Bell 1976: IX; Kleinsteuber 1999: 22; Drucker 2011: 17ff.; Masuda 1981: 3). Information and knowledge processing dominate as a form of production and becomes the decisive growth driver of the ongoing industry. However, this also means that the information society as a whole relies on both the necessary knowledge being made available and access to information simplified (cf. Tully 1994: 19). Overall, dealing with information becomes so much a part of our private and professional life that information as an object of action becomes the paradigm of the social constitution. As a result, societies emerging focus is no longer on material objects, but on information activities, which occupy a significant part of human life, both at work and at leisure (cf. Klotz 2009: 17).

All in all the concept of information society gained enormous significance from politics during the 1990s. During that time the information society experienced its renaissance primarily as a political help concept to cover the most visible changes in prevailing societies. Its importance was emphasized by converging trends such as individualization and globalization, with related technological advances (cf. Kleinsteuber 1999: 26; Bode 1997: 25f., Steinbicker: 7). Politicians, business leaders and policymakers around the globe have taken the information society idea to their hearts during that time. They assumed that information and communication technologies would have a decisive influence on the design of the information society of the 21st century (cf. Glowalla 1996: 27). Overall, support for the further development of the Information Society at the end of the 20th century was seen as an overall policy field, nationally, supranationally, and internationally or globally In this way, an adaptation to a global information society should be promoted (cf. Klotz 2009: 5; Webster 2006: 2).

3.2.1. The Rise of ICT

Information and communications technologies mean the infrastructure and components that enable modern computing. Although there is no universal definition of ICT, the term is generally accepted to mean all devices, networking components, applications and systems that combined allow people and organizations to interact in the digital world (cf. Rouse 2018). In terms of the concept of an information society, it is related to modernity and progress orientation. As far as concretization is concerned, as already mentioned in the previous chapter, the advantages of new information and communication techniques are emphasized. They have been described as the guiding technology and the epitome of structural change. Moreover, they are paradigmatic for the new knowledge-based industries and play an important role in the transformation of the division of labor, organization and administration (cf. Steinbicker 2011: 9; Berthoud 2003: 388).

In the literature at the time of the emergence of the information society in the second half of the 20th century, it was often associated with Telecommunication in the course of the development of ICT, which was

said to spread very quickly using the new techniques (cf. Kleinsteuber 1999: 27f.). But also emerging technologies in computing or the early stage of the Internet have to be mentioned. On the whole, those responsible in politics and business assumed that information and communication technologies will have a decisive influence on the design of the information society of the 21st century. To this day, it can not be denied, and there are always new and unexpected technical possibilities. The progressive mechanization of human communication is still an ongoing process (cf. Glowalla 1996: 27).
For example, computer or internet-based ICT are already omnipresent today. Data networks are being expanded and becoming denser. Information and communication technologies are increasingly determining our lives. For example, factory buildings, machine tools, production lines and entire production areas are already automated. Traders, suppliers, banks, and customers are networked through information systems. State authorities manage citizens in huge databases. Even private life gets more and more penetrated by these technologies. It can be assumed that this rise of ICT will continue in the future. These technologies and the digital economy have the potential to transform the lives of billions of people, and by that also the information society. This will also cause massive changes in communication relationships. Advocates of this developments argue that society can be relieved of technology by doing boring, heavy or dangerous work. Life and work become more pleasant. In addition, human error sources can be eliminated, economic productivity increased and more information and knowledge made available to everyone in society. However, this technical development also involves many risks and can result in enormous damage in cases of abuse of ICT (cf. Roßnagel et al 2009: 5ff.; Telecommunication Union 2017). Regarding the current market volume of the ICT industry, as well as the qualification of ICT as a cross-sectional technology supports the concept of an information society. Nevertheless, the investigations of these facts with regard to their validity or reliability are partly called into question by a few scholars (cf. Klotz 2009: 14 ff.).

All in all, it can be summarized that today's use of information and communication technologies forms is an important basis of a modern information society. This is illustrated, among other things, by the demonstrated everyday use of these technologies. Also, the ongoing digitalization is accompanied by further penetration of most societal spheres with ICT, which continuously changes the information society.

3.2.2. Employment Inside the Information Society

This chapter will illustrate how employment within the information society look like and how it can be characterized from the perspective of theory.
As mentioned, the concept of the information society based on many fundamental changes in the society and revolutionary developments, especially in information and communication technologies. Computers, the Internet, and smartphones among other inventions affect the social environment, live and employment in modern information societies. Since not all of the impact can be captured in the course of this chapter, it will characterize a few. This includes the importance of information and the so-called knowledge worker because he frequently appears on the basis of the literature on the information society and is seen as an essential figure in the context of employment. In the course of this research, he should serve as a metaphor for the effects of information society on work in society and will be described in the last part of this chapter.

Based on the research so far, the rise of ICT, Information, and knowledge have become keywords in the context of the information society. Their impact on employment of the information society is significant. For example, the use of computer-based work equipment is developing fast in the last two decades. In the 1990s it was already recognized that at the place where predominantly information is processed, these computer-based work tools have considerable influence on the quantity and quality of the work. So nowadays the entire information society is based on the computers, mobile phones or other information and communication technology devices for professional purposes. So dealing with information becomes a big part of peoples professional life, and Information as an object of action becomes the paradigm of the social constitution. An information society emerges, in which no more acts on material objects are in the foreground, but information activities occupy a substantial portion of human employment, whether at work or leisure (cf. Klotz 2009: 14ff., Dostal 1995: 528). All of these changes and the use of powerful endpoints are the technical basis for a fundamental change in social behaviors, interpersonal relationships, and work. These are also increasingly shaped by the human-machine interaction, the immediate social contact decreases (cf. Klotz 2009: 14ff.; Klotz 2003: 157ff.; Makridakis 2017:19ff.).

In the course of this mentioned technological change also the employment structures within the society changed and should be described briefly. At the end of the last century, emerging tech like computers and the Internet raised the relative productivity of higher-skilled workers. Routine-intensive occupations that focused on predictable, easily-programmable tasks were particularly vulnerable to replacement by new technologies. These occupations included for example switchboard operators, filing clerks, travel agents, and assembly line workers. Some of these occupations were virtually eliminated and demand for others reduced. Based on research it is suggested that technological innovation over this period increased the productivity of those engaged in abstract thinking, creative tasks, and problem-solving and was therefore at least partially responsible for the substantial growth in jobs employing such traits. So a shifting demand towards more skilled labor raised the relative income of this group, contributing to rising inequality (cf. U.S. Government 2016).

As part of the modern information society, the newly created jobs and thus new types of workers were described in second half of the 20th century with terms like knowledge or information worker. From a theoretical perspective, the majority of people in the information society work in professions, which are characterized by the fact that almost all activities are based on information. From a theoretical perspective, the majority of people in the information society work in professions, which are characterized by the fact that almost all activities based on information. They include the collection and acquisition of data, their evaluation, and processing. Based on the concept of the information society developed so far, it is argued that most people work in such occupations. Corresponding information and media literacy become necessary in order to be able to counteract the flood of information and the resulting explosion of knowledge and to be able to use the increasing range of information for its own benefit (cf. Klotz 2009: 14 ff., Arriaga 1985: 272). This leads to a new type of work, which can be described as knowledge. It is differentiated from other forms of work by its emphasis on non-routine problem solving that requires a combination of convergent and divergent thinking (cf. Reinhardt 2011; 150ff.).

Based on the concept of the information society, the following part of the chapter will introduce as already mentioned at the beginning of this chapter the term knowledge worker. From a theoretical perspective, the so-called knowledge worker is an often quoted metaphor for characterizing live and work on an individual level in the information

society and still provides a substantial part of the sociology of professions (cf. Svarc 2016: 398). The literature on knowledge workers offers many different definitions and ideas, but for this research, they simplified to three approaches. First conceptual approaches, second job content approaches and third data (industry) driven approaches. Conceptual approaches explain knowledge worker from the complex point of view. For example employees' importance for an organization, his style of work with knowledge, or education (cf. Davenport 2005, Drucker 1954, Lowe 2002, Reboul et al 2006). Data (industry) driven approaches understand as knowledge worker all those, who work in particular organizations or particular sectors or institutions (cf. Brinkley et al. 2009, Sveiby 1997). Job content approaches interpret knowledge worker as people who do a certain type of job. Across the different approaches, authors understand knowledge worker as a person who mainly creates, applies, and distributes knowledge. Employers highly regard him for his innovation and creativity. Also, he is driven by accomplishment and highly committed to what he is doing. A knowledge workers position requires continuous learning and improving (cf. Toffler 1990; Spira 2008; Reich 1992; Kidd 1994; Mladkova et al. 2015: 769f.; Mladkova 2015: 179). Likewise, this type of worker is characterized by a pronounced social competence, which manifests itself above all in the combination of social, professional competences. The typology of knowledge worker roles suggested by them are a coordinator, helper, learner, researcher, problem-solver, networker, organizer, and communicator (cf. Reinhardt 2011: 150ff.; Klotz 2009 S.19 ff.).
Overall, the knowledge of the knowledge worker represents his means of production, which he can dispose freely of. Thus, knowledge workers are mobile and independent (cf. Drucker 1999: 37; Drucker 1959; Davenport 2005). Drucker sees his productivity as the most valuable asset in the 21st century. If this is unfolded, innovations can emerge. For this research, it should be assumed that the main characteristics of this concept of the information worker still exist today, although it is not uncontroversial.

All in all, it can be summarized that modern employment in the information society is characterised by the use of ICT, the importance of information and the metaphor of the so-called knowledge worker.

3.2.3. The Information Economy

Based on the concept of the information society developed so far, this chapter will concentrate on its economic dimension. It will characterise the concept of the so-called information economy, also referred to the term knowledge-based information economy, post-industrial economy and the newly created information sector. In general, it characterizes an economy in which information, knowledge, and services are more valuable than manufacturing. The technological respectively digital developments associated with the revolution in instruments of knowledge and the growth in ICT or computer-based systems has accelerated the shift of industrialized countries from manufacturing-based economies toward service-based economies (cf. Cambridge Dictionary 2018; Porat 1998: 101ff.).

Knowledge has been at the heart of economic growth and the gradual rise in levels of social well-being since time immemorial. The ability to invent and innovate, that is, to create new knowledge and ideas that are then embodied in products, processes, and organizations, has always served to fuel development. There have always been organizations or institutions capable of creating and disseminating knowledge. However, information economy or knowledge-based economy is a recently coined term. Its use is meant to signify a change from the economies of earlier periods, more a „sea change“ than a sharp discontinuity (cf. David 2003: 20).

The first calculations for the Information Economy had been developed by economists in the USA. The pioneering American work on this concept was carried out by Machlup in 1962. In a seminal investigation of those engaged in the production and distribution of knowledge, he measured the expenditures on knowledge production and its importance to the economy of the united states at this time (cf. Trauth 2000: 6; Karvalics 2007: 6; Machlup 1962). Based on Machlups concept of this knowledge industry, Porats follow-up study of the American information economy in the 1970th added greater refinement to this emerging concept and was repeated in other countries. Porat constructed an independent fourth sector, the so-called information sector (cf. Klotz 2009: 8f.; Porat 1977). For that, he divides the workforce into four sectors. The information, agriculture, industry, and service sector. There is no longer any conflation of the information and service sectors. Both are distinct, and the former has outstripped the latter. Porat figures out, that this information sector in 1967 accounted for nearly 50 percent of US GNP and more

than 50 percent of wages and salaries, and affirms that it is in that sense that they have become an information economy (cf. Bell 1980: 521; Duff 1998: 382f.; Porat 1977).
All in all Machlup and Porat assumed that employment was in the process of epoch-making redeployment and that shortly most of the employees will act as information workers. This process has been identified worldwide. Led by the US, other highly developed states followed. The figures presented in this context were based on the assumption that more and more occupational activities will focus on information and the processing of knowledge. For example, it has been claimed that in the US in 1967, more than half of the workforce worked in the information sector (cf. Kleinsteuber 1999: 21f.; Porat 1977).

This change in the economy is also essential to Bell. The primary source for Bell's mentioned theory of post-industrialism is a short chapter of „The Coming of Post-Industrial Society" entitled „From goods to services: the changing shape of the economy". Bell declares that it is clear if an industrial society is defined as a goods-producing society - if the manufacturer is central in shaping the character of its labor force - then the United States at this time is no longer an industrial society. His evidence for this strong verdict was based on a significant growth of the service sector and a more or less contemporaneous decline of the manufacturing sector. Whereas employment in the goods-producing sector increased from 10.63 million in 1870 to 25.6 million in 1940, and was projected to reach 31.6 million in 1980, service employment in the USA went up much more rapidly over the same period, from 2.99 million in 1870 to 24.25 million in 1940 and 67.98 million (projected) in 1980. Bell also provides percentage figures, and these indicated that the goods-producing proportion of the US workforce dropped from 51% in 1947 to 31.7% in 1980, while the service sector increased from 49% to 68.4% (cf. Duff 1998: 376f.; Bell 1973: 133).

The main characteristic of this new information economy is that people and their jobs are best understood as service related, as the provision of information, the deployment of knowledge. After Porat most of these people new work is related to the term information labor, which bases on information activities (cf. May 2000: 5ff.).
This development and the associated characteristics of the economy form the basis of the concept Information Economy within this chapter. Based on the previously outlined concept, the industry can be divided after Machlup into five sub-divisions: Education, research and develop-

ment, the media of communication, information machines and information services. From today's perspective, these areas have also undergone further development in the past. However, it is believed that these five differentiated areas are still useful for macro-level categorization of an industry for today's analysis purposes.

3.3. Information Society and AI

The question this chapter raises is how AI generally fits into the developed framework of the information society and its economic dimension? Where are the theoretical starting points and what possible changes are most relevant in the face of the previous chapters?

Emerging technologies and opportunities in artificial intelligence are based on the Rise of ICT, as illustrated in the last chapter as one basic characteristic of a modern information society.

As an ongoing and longer-term trend, AI seems to be a product of the information society itself based on the technological development. More and more information is generated which in turn is evaluated and transformed through AI, creating ways to turn information into productive use. AI could further help to assist humans in dealing with ever increasing complexities of tasks, processes and value chains. In terms of a machine-human interaction, the individuals would only need to understand certain aspects and limited information in the process, other aspects would be handled by machines. As a consequence, AI might relieve the problem of persons being overburdened by huge quantities and complex information.

Further, the rise of new opportunities might be accelerated, often labeled as the "exponential character" of new technologies (cf. Dörner 2017). Enhanced quantitative digital infrastructure combined with qualitative technical innovation are decisive for this process. There is a consensus in the literature that AI will continuously impact all our ways to live and work. The question is, how vast and deep will the impact be.

As illustrated in chapter 3.2.2, the knowledge worker will be strongly affected. Assuming that the category of „knowledge worker" will remain a valid one, it must be assumed that the typical job and task profile for knowledge workers will change throughout the process of digitalization and the more under AI. Knowledge workers will work in the so-called information sector. As a logical consequence, they might become the prime and key resource handling the raw material information. With the help of Artificial intelligence, humans could make more efficient deci-

sions sector specific outputs could be increased. However, in order to achieve this, each algorithm required to handle data and information needs to be tailored carefully to existing data, and the objectives pursued. This requires considerable human expertise for the knowledge or information worker in machine learning and large datasets to train algorithms. Obviously, the demands of the knowledge worker will rise, and education and learning must be increased and shifted to meet these demands.
The current developments in AI seem able to produce two options. First, an increased human-machine interaction increased the productivity of the information worker. The limited human ability to pay attention to, handle and process data and perform tasks related here is augmented. If AI overcomes human limitations and boundaries, more information can be processed and used to make better-informed decisions, faster and more efficiently. The productivity of the information worker rises.

Another possibility is that exponential technology like AI replaces even the most highly qualified knowledge worker. Thus, the information society itself could replace humans in workplaces. It is maybe be assumed, and this would have to be verified by evidence in the future, that AI alone in some segments or even across economic segments produces better work results than even the most skilled knowledge workers can achieve. As a consequence, the conflict between labor and machine-generated output are augmented. Likely, jobs requiring the least skill and knowledge sets are hit first. It is not a new phenomenon that the information society poses the question of a deep conflict between highly qualified knowledge workers on the one hand and marginalized service sector employees on the other side, as Drucker argues (cf. Steinbicker 2011: 9f.). Almost ironically, this conflict could cease under the following scenario: Imagine – theoretically - not a single human would be able to compete with AI, each task and job would be better handled by AI. If so, all humans would be equally affected, the conflict between high and low skilled workers would disappear. From today's perspective, a more likely scenario would be that the conflict will materialize between strong AI and knowledge workers for the job, the low skilled workforce segment would be out of the equation of job finding, already replaced by AI.
In other words, instead of „transformation“, i.e. a switch from resources from one sector to the other, a situation like this would lead to idle human resources, further caused by a huge skill gap. And this on a massive scale. An imaginable scenario like this caused by strong AI will strongly

influence the so-called information society if human labor would increasingly disappear.

Besides of AI also concurrent advances in the internet of things, big data analytics, cloud computing is coming up and will enable tremendous innovations in the information society (cf. International Telecommunication Union 2017). They all together could lead more likely to transforming of business, government, and society fundamentally.

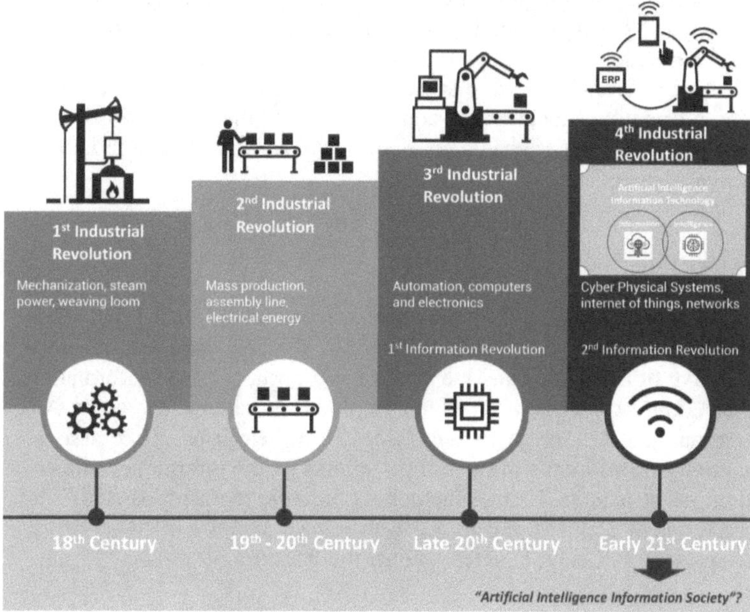

Figure V: Artificial Intelligence Information Society. Source: Own graphic.

The illustration reflects an Artificial Intelligence Information Society, a future envisioned by the risks and opportunities brought about by AI and the infiltration of automated machines and computers at all levels of the economy (cf. Lee 2016).

As already indicated, in addition to the many positive aspects, these outlined developments also raise a number of critical questions that cannot be illustrated in this chapter. However, to prevent, in particular, the part of the potentially massive adverse effects, it is necessary to shape the future technical possibilities of ICT and their applications by using criteria of so-called social compatibility. In this context, the question arises how much adverse technological side effects does an information society tolerate and when will it be threatening for a nation on a massive scale? Moreover, how precisely should technical alternatives be weighed to prevent society from being hurt too much? (cf. Roßnagel et al. 1990: 6). Many ethical issues open up in this context, even they can not further be elaborated in this chapter.

Nonetheless, the need to address fundamental issues with technology assessment within the information society is essential to control technological development. In the latter part of the research, reference should be made to this again. It seems worthwhile to study the change and future of work within the socio-economic impact of AI. The future of the information economy, the consequences for the information society and the action requirements on a political macro level have to be further investigated.

3.4. Hypotheses

Based on the argument put forward so far, it can be concluded that "Rise of ICT" made AI as a technology possible, this technological development gave birth to AI. Thus we said AI is a product of the information society. And first signs of changing employment patterns driven by AI-driven automatization can be witnessed. From here it is safe to assume that strong AI will have even stronger effects on the information society and on job structures. Using Machlup's economic segments as study objects, we shall seek to conduct a deeper impact analysis in chapter five. The analysis will be conducted against the background of two hypotheses:

(a) The occupational structures resulting from todays information societies will be affected by massive labor market changes due to strong AI. As a consequence, AI has the potential to disrupt the main subdivisions of the information economy.

(b) The beginning of strong AI seems to be the key for the information society to work more efficiently with the upcoming almost unmeasurable amounts of data and their complexity. AI can perform better than every single knowledge worker could do. As a consequence, the disruptive impact of strong AI will change the concept of knowledge workers as well as their relevance as their range of tasks within the Information Economy.

The validity of these two hypotheses shall be discussed with the help of the use-cases within sub-segments of the information economy. The goal is to evaluate how deep economies within the information societies are influenced by strong AI.

4. Methodology

The methodological approach within this thesis can be characterized as a two-step analysis framework. The first analysis will concentrate on a micro-level perspective on industry segments, and the second one on a rather political macro-level. For that, the concept of the Information Economy as the economic dimension of the information society shall form the generic base of the methodological approach. As already discussed in the third chapter the Information Economy concept is widely acknowledged as a way to describe highly developed large economies. Further, it can be adjusted to the purpose of this investigation and enriched by the notion of strong AI. To then attempt to estimate the impact of strong AI on different industry sectors, Machlup's segmentation of economies in the information society age should be used: Education, Information Services, Information Machines, The Media of Communication, Research and Development. These five segments shall be used as research objects to discuss the impact strong AI might have on them beyond weak AI or common digitization trends. The special notion is placed on employment and labor skills since. For that, it will cover qualitative research methods and seek to investigate the effects of strong AI based on recent studies and additional literature such as available online news articles between 2017 and 2018.
While the first analysis based on Machlup takes a rather "micro" view on industry segments, the second step of the analysis will change to a rather macro-political view. If many economic sectors are affected, what implications may arise for the entire information society and for the political sphere? Again, hypotheses are developed, arguing that actions are required to alleviate the effects of AI.

By using this method, the thesis then attempts to draw conclusions and first initial recommendations to policy makers. There might be many complex and intertwined ones, not feasible to handle in this thesis. All in all, this methodological approach will contribute to this goal by discussing the political possibilities of actions in the final part of the research guided by the hypotheses.

5. Analysis of AI in the Information Economy

This chapter seeks to develop a framework to assess how strong AI will impact the Information Economy. The conceptual approach here for consists of the assumption that Machlup's description of the Information Economy is still very much valid. Surely, changes have occurred (also due to the development of information technology) in the different segments described by Machlup. But on a macro view, the concept remains intact and the five segments of concept shall be investigated, which are: Education, Information Services, Information Machines, The Media of Communication, Research and Development. Within each of these industries, one sector or sub-segment will be investigated. A precondition for the investigations is that sufficient literature is available to conduct a qualitative analysis.
It will be attempted to show, which and how many of Machlup's segments will experience strong impacts from AI in the future. This further requires analyzing the technology deployed within the segments or industrial sectors and how many fields of applications for new AI technologies are present. An assessment of the suitability and probability of workforce replacement by strong AI is equally based on literature.

The following analysis uses three expressions with the following meaning: Short-term describes a timespan less than five years, mid-term means five to fifteen years and long-term should be used as a synonym for more than fifteen years.

5.1. Education

In the wake of the digitalization and AI focused automation, there are discussions on how to revolutionize the education sector with emerging technologies, whether gamifying instructional materials or expanding access to knowledge via massive open online courses. Based on recent reports the market of education technology acceleration will be hugely dictated by the global education expenditure market, as education becomes increasingly more expensive. In fact, the market stands now at over five trillion dollars, 8x the size of the software market and 3x size of the media and entertainment industry, yet education is only two percent digitized. Education technologies, broadly defined as the use of computers or other technology to enhance teaching, are becoming a global phenomenon, and as distribution and platforms scale internationally, the outlined market is projected to grow at 17 percent per year, up to 252 billion dollars by 2020. Even private investment in educational technology grew 32 percent annually from 2011 through 2015, rising to 4.5 billion dollars globally. AI's share of these flows is likely to increase because especially strong artificial intelligence technologies might be well suited to achieve crucial education objectives, such as enhancing teaching efficiency and effectiveness, providing education for everybody, and developing the skills that will be essential in the 21st century (cf. Newswire Europe 2016; McKinsey 2017: 65).

Education as one of the primary industries of the developed information economy is already distinguished in the book „The production and distribution of knowledge in the united states" by Fritz Machlup in the 20th century. The exact characteristics and main drivers of the industry changed significantly in the last decades, but it can be assumed that the basic categorization of the information economy itself is also applicable in modern days. By that one important subindustry is still job education, which seems very important concerning the knowledge worker explained in chapter three. Usually, analysis requires further distinctions. With regard to the production and acquisition of knowledge while working on a job, for example in the case of an employee of a business firm, one should distinguish between training on the job provided by the employer and learning on the job on the part of the employee without any training activities arranged by the employer (cf. Machlup 1962: 51f.). Furthermore, higher education seems to be important to train the knowledge worker constantly.
Education in jobs and higher education should be the analysis object within this chapter. After a short introduction, the focus will be on how the different sub-industries of education could develop with emerging possibilities of strong AI.

Following recent reports by Pearson in collaboration with University College London Knowledge Lab or McKinsey, the impact of AI on the education sector in the future will be significant. They note that today's model-based adaptive systems are increasingly transparent, allowing educators to understand how a system arrived at a next-step decision and rendering them more effective tools for classroom teaching (cf. Faggella 2017).

The first important aspect to look at, are virtual tutors powered by AI, which could possibly disrupt the education sector in the future. Strong AI is supposed to personalize and optimize teaching and learning at all. So-called adaptive learning solutions aim to address the limitations of conventional classroom teaching. Accordingly, personalizing lesson plans to the student or worker existing knowledge, particular learning preferences, and individual progress could be methods. Instead of delivering one lesson to an entire group, which can leave behind struggling participants or disengage fast learners, adaptive learning claims to deliver the right content, at the right time, in the best way to every single person. AI could easily improve adaptive learning and personalized teaching by identifying factors or indicators of successful learning for every single person. Not only monitoring such variables as the number of breaks or unconcentrated moments during a lesson or the amount of time needed to answer a question is a way to enforce the individual learning progress. In addition, computer vision and deep learning could call in new information such as mouse movements, eye tracking, and sentiment analysis, delivering a deeper insight on everybody's individual performance, mindset, or cognitive ability. This data could be used to support students in real time.

Implemented at scale, AI-enabled adaptive learning could restructure higher education and education on the job. By that, it could mean an end for traditional testing systems and measure academic abilities and achievement in a more nuanced way. Class formats would give more room for individuals to learn according to their preferences and needs, with teachers focusing less on lecturing and more on coaching, aided by prescriptive analytics to choose the most effective methods. Finally, the use of strong artificial intelligence at this point could empower learners by providing them with control over how fast or in which way they learn best, and the lifelong feedback of one's own cognitive and behavioral preferences. Strong AI could easily encompass all of the individual learning styles and provide a customized plan for each person after getting to know the learning behaviour of a student and how he learns. Along with this plan, the programs imagable as a so-called individual AI-powered tutor could help to craft more specific and even more realistic goals for every single learner (cf. Avery 2018; McKinsey 2017: 67; Lynch 2018; Turbot 2017; Maney 2017). Because educational software is adapted to individual needs, there is evidence to suggest that intelligent tutoring systems perform as well, if not better, than individual human tutors for many students (cf. Faggella 2017; TeachThought Staff 2017; Phillips 2018). On the one hand, deep learning algorithms could predict outcomes and prescribe accurate solutions. On the other hand, they could explain how the algorithm itself reached its conclusion and helped retro-engineer drivers of educational success. This will allow individual learners and workers to reflect on their cognitive abilities and understand their optimal learning setting by getting constructive feedback. Empowered by strong AI, individuals could build their own virtual robot teachers and learning partners to help them navigate lifelong learning experiences.

The promise of strong AI at this point of consideration is to use digital tools as a cognitive window into each person's minds and help tailor learning to maximize individuals potential (cf. McKinsey 2017: 67f.; Pearson 2016: 23).

Based on unleashing personalized learning also the learning experience will change entirely for everybody involved in education, even teaching in higher education requires a reconsideration of educators and pedagogies role (cf. Popenici/ Kerr 2017: 11). Every teacher and educator could benefit from virtual guidance. In an information age dominated by digital content, teachers must shift from a sage on a stage to the guides on the side. In other words, coaching might be more important than teaching in the digital age because virtual environments have already allowed teachers to make this shift. Coaches help students by setting their own goals and reflect on their growth in the environment, while also setting up more lengthy open-ended projects to ensure learners apply the content to real-world situations. This blended environment allows human learners and machines to work symbiotically (cf. Wagner 2018).

Arguing that one of the teachers most valuable asset is time, strong AI could help them to spend their time more wisely, efficient and goal-oriented. Before the onset of AI, much of their time was spent developing and delivering content in a rigid, inflexible curriculum framework (cf. Wagner 2018). Nowadays AI is starting being able to do some of the basic activities in education and mundane duties that consume a teachers time. Also, routine grading is a task that eats up a teachers time. Strong AI can easily score hundreds of multiple-choice tests with precision accuracy. Furthermore, it is becoming more and more possible for AI to grade written essays, or oral presentations and simplify the process of grading in this way. All in all, it will take AI far less time to do so than a

human. In return, the elimination of time-consuming grading tasks presents the opportunity for educators to pay more attention to creating a better classroom lesson or concentrating on the students and trainees themselves. This focus can be seen as a value-adding and more important task connected to the human teacher role (cf. Phillips 2018; Lynch 2018; TeachThought Staff 2017; Narula 2018). This requires specific skills, such as emotional intelligence, creativity, and communication, that are beyond machines current capabilities. That is why the human teachers should concentrate on staying good at these things. Instead of supervising and answering routine questions or taking attendance could be seen as another time-consuming administrative task of a teacher, which could be done by an AI system in the future as well. Natural language, computer vision, and deep learning could help replace teachers also in answering students routine questions or acting as tutorial supervisors.
AI could also give teachers additional support in forming the most effective classes by applying machine learning algorithms to data from learners education profile, surveys or social media. Anyway, in most cases, the upcoming improvements in the field of AI will shift the traditional role of teachers to that of facilitators (cf. TeachThought Staff 2017; McKinsey: 68f.; Houser 2017).

The improvements towards virtual assistance and virtual teachers will increase significantly in the next years. Also in situations if it is not possible to have an experienced advisor, AI could be the experienced teacher, powered by learnings from big data AI can fill the gaps in subject areas in which a teacher does not have a particular expertise or helps by training teachers when there is a skill shortage in the job market (cf. Avery 2018; Houser 2017; Pearson 2016). With a much wider reach, AI-assisted teaching could also have a significant impact in third world countries and remote locations by supporting two key enablers of teaching, which can be described as coaching and assessing (cf. McKinsey: 68f.). Furthermore introducing AI to educational settings will benefit learners of all ages. For example for many subjects, as people get older, they are not willing to take that learning risk where they are confused. For example, Bill Gates emphasizes within this context:

> „The idea that you could talk to a virtual advisor that would understand different misconceptions and arbitrary linguistics around it, that will certainly come in the next decade." (Avery 2018).

Another major asset of strong artificial intelligence might be the ability to know more exact details and having higher expertise than every human educator. Because trial and error is a critical part of learning, not knowing the answer is paralyzing for learners or educators itself. This could change with strong AI as well. A further promising aspect is an increase in flexibility. Individuals can start learning from anywhere in the world at any time, by using AI systems, software, and support. These kinds of programs taking the place of certain types of classroom instruction, strong AI may replace teachers in some instances (cf. TeachThought Staff 2017).
The last relevant aspect of strong AI within this chapter might be taking a key role in better connecting education systems and labor markets, which could mean benefits for every single knowledge worker and the society at all. Also connecting talent with opportunities in the job market, improve recruitment results or enabling education systems to meet the needs of future employers better can be seen as further advantages by strong AI. Furthermore, the technology itself could be used by governments to forecast detailed job-market demand more accurately and steer educational institutions to adapt their curricula and approaches accordingly, making sure students have the skills required to fill those jobs (cf. McKinsey 2017: 65ff.).

As analyzed so far, strong AI solutions will have the potential to structurally change education on jobs, higher education or education at all. As already analyzed, AI might raise its quality by making it more personalized or efficient as well for the learners as for the educators (cf. Pearson 2016: 21). However, the realm of teaching and learning in higher education, for example, might also present a very different set of challenges. At the moment AI solutions relate to tasks that can be automated but can not be yet envisaged as a solution for more complex tasks of higher learning (cf. Popenici/ Kerr 2017: 11). Anyway, further developments in the field of strong AI are important to look at. By giving an outlook, the most relevant development in the next years might be the human-machine integration.

> "AI is doing some of the very labor-intensive data collection and analysis that is best done by technology, leaving the teacher to do the human interaction that's much better done by humans (...) You keep the bit that the humans are particularly good at, and then you try and automate the support within that system." (Avery 2018).

In the early future human educators still have to concentrate on things that are beyond machines current capabilities. These are for example value-adding tasks, emotional intelligence, creativity, interpersonal communication or building relationships.
Not to be overlooked is the apparent fear of some scholars that human educators and teachers will be replaced by strong AI technologies in the coming decade. AI will most likely not replace most of the human educators in short-term or mid-term but will serve as an invaluable extension of the human expert, helping teachers to more effectively meet the diverse needs of many learners simultaneously (cf. Faggella 2017; Houser 2017). Another fact against the mentioned human replacement in education is, that currently, only a few percents of the education sector are digitalized, which in turn can be seen as a basis for strong AI. After the educational sector is more digitalized, the development of human replacement could speed up.

It may be concluded that profound changes arising from strong AI have to be expected in the education sector, even only sub-segments have been investigated here.

5.2. Information Services

Information Services mean this part of the information economy where agencies or departments are responsible for providing processed or published information on specific topics to an organization's internal users, its customers, or the general public (cf. Business Dictionry 2018). Machlup describes it as an important industry for knowledge production, which is fundamental for the information society. He describes to understand by knowledge-production any human or human-induced activity effectively designed to create, alter, or confirm in a human mind a meaningful apperception, awareness, cognizance, or consciousness of whatever it may be: „The activity of telling anybody anything, by word of mouth or in writing, is knowledge-production in this sense. A person exclusively engaged in this activity belongs to a knowledge- producing occupation. A number of firms exclusively engaged in selling information or advice belong to a knowledge-producing industry.“ (Machlup 1962: 323).
In his book „The production and distribution of knowledge in the united states“ he made a solid empirical analysis of the existing industry because it is one of the main parts of the information economy. The most essential subdivisions after Machlup are professional knowledge services

including legal services, engineering and architectural services, accounting and auditing, and medical services. Other are intelligence service of wholesale traders or financial services. All of them are specialized in producing or selling information and advice (cf. Machlup 1962: 323f.).

The ongoing chapter will concentrate on the financial services because it might be still one of the most important and developed industry for the use of AI within the information services nowadays. The primary goal is to look at the market and potential of AI within this field guided by the basic hypotheses of Analyse I and the following questions. How does AI revolutionize this specific sector? What are the supposed consequences of an AI adaption within this industry?
The market for AI in financial services is expected to grow from 1.3 billion dollars in 2017 to 7.4 billion dollars in 2022, at a Compound Annual Growth Rate of 40 percent, according to research and markets. A reason might be that the financial services industry is facing both numerous opportunities to innovate and challenges ahead that will determine the future landscape of the industry post-disruption (cf. Fraser 2017). Many applications of AI within this field already exist. It has been creeping into financial services under a variety of names, assisted in no small part by related technologies such as digitalization, interactive voice response and image recognition or data mining for personal identity validation (cf. Narrativ Science 2017: 5). On the one hand, the adoption of AI use cases has been driven by both supply factors, such as technological advances and the availability of financial sector data and infrastructure. On the other hand, by demand factors, such as profitability needs, competition with other firms, and the demands of financial regulation (cf. Financial Stability Board 2017: 5). Nowadays financial services companies have been working on creating real-life AI use cases and are exploring new opportunities with hopes that strong AI could both cut costs and boost revenues (cf. Donovan: 2017; Williams-Grut 2017). However, it is estimated that it will revolutionize finance through the ability to combine structured and unstructured data and provide precise market analysis (cf. Baker 2018).
All in all, AI seems to be supposed to optimize financial services as an extensive solution for existing challenges. In the following part, a few concrete ways how especially strong AI could transform the financial service industry in the next years should be analysed.

The first aspect is the enhancing customer engagement. At a time when the financial services industry needs to become increasingly fo-

cused on creating better customer experiences, the importance of high-quality and personalized communications is very important nowadays. For example, by using deep neural networks, different companies have already developed a conversational AI platform for financial institutions that is like a more advanced „Siri for your finances". It supports the same natural language flow that a customer possibly has with his personal banker (cf. Chowdhry 2018).
The imagination of strong AI can also definitely help to tackle this mission of enhancing customer engagement, both automatically and at scale. This personalized communications or advice as enabled by AI would be extended in several ways. For example, the customers own robo-advisors in the wealth management space that provide automated, algorithm-based portfolio management advice without the help of a human counterpart. In this case, AI also automates the so-called „Know Your Customer Processes" for the mentioned wealth management.

Also in terms of investment and asset management. AI is already starting to optimize this process that takes hours, or that often results in a human error (cf. Narrative Science 2017: 7; Bhardwaj 2018; Fraser 2017, Bashforth 2018). Research shows that evidence-based algorithms predict the future more accurately than human forecasters.

> "Artifcial intelligence can help people make faster, better, and cheaper decisions. But you have to be willing to collaborate with the machine, and not just treat it as either a servant or an overlord." (Bhardwaj 2018).

An advanced level of AI and human collaboration could help human experts to identify issues and save time. The market size of robo-advisors, for example, seems to increase productivity as well and could eventually approach the so-called assets under management of the entire asset management industry in time. Similarly, AI-enabled personal finance intelligence applications are helping consumers to manage their finances, analyze their spending, automate tax form filing, or making financial recommendations with a business model not predicated to generating fees from investments. This sketched automation of traditional retail functions is made possible mainly through the creation of smart assistants and voice recognition technology (cf. Bashforth 2018; Fraser 2017). It also improves the targeting of messages at all and could end up with providing better customer support through AI and computer-based customer services (cf. Technative 2017). In the field of customer support, especially the current state of the art of conversational AI for virtual assistance like chatbots helps companies to achieve more productivity and customers to transact or to solve problems faster.

So a further use case of AI in financial services is to help customers in the field of decision support also by reducing essential risks. Personal assistance and robo-advisory services can help the consumer to spend and invest more wisely by giving augmented recommendations (cf. Narrativ Science 2017: 9f.; Bashforth 2018; Technative 2017; Bhardwaj 2018; Javelosa/ Houser 2017). But it can help the companies in the same way to minimize their own risks. For example in the fields of credit scoring the decisionmakers could use AI for robust credit lending applications to achieve faster, more accurate risk assessment, using machine intelligence to factor in the character and capacity of applicants (cf. Sigmoidal 2018; Financial Stability Board 2017: 11ff).
Another famous use case of strong AI is being used in automated fraud detection and reduction, as well as anti-money laundering and anti-terrorist financing compliance monitoring.

> "In most cases, the daily transaction volume is far too high for humans to manually review each transaction. Instead, AI is used to create systems that learn what types of transactions are fraudulent." (Narula 2018).

To reduce the fraudulent transactions is a huge benefit. But these fraud detection technologies are certainly not new. Regarding strong AI the innovative aspect is that AI and machine learning can mimic the associative memory of the human brain to identify likely fraud with an infinitely larger data set. Especially deep learning could further reduce fraud as it can take in thousands of variables versus a few dozens (cf. Fraser 2017: 4f.; Bashforth 2018). It is important because the most significant challenges in the financial and banking field are the complexity involved in identifying fraud. By leveraging better AI platforms and solutions, companies could automate the analysis of massive amounts of data, which mean to fraudulent actors and other threats can be recognized and dealt with faster (cf. Bhardwaj 2018). They could also be developed into a predictive cybersecurity monitoring and response systems (cf. Bashforth 2018).

All in all the client experience within the financial services can be fundamentally transformed through the power of strong AI. Morrissey, a technology strategist of Microsoft, emphasize that the future is an intelligent bank for example, where technology can predict seamlessly what the client needs next and empower them. Also, the next generation will demand new levels of personalization and frictionless experiences (cf. Morrissey 2017). In mid-term these improvements could end up in using much more bots then human employees. For example, to improve the targeting of messages or to provide better customer support and computer-based customer services, AI can be seen as a job destroyer in the financial services. It may be concluded that profound changes arising from strong AI have to be expected for the entire industry, even only a subsegment has been investigated here.

5.3. Information Machines

Machlup further subdivides the sector Information Machines. He distinguishes between Information Machines for Knowledge Industries, Instruments for Measurement, Observation, and Control, Office Information Machines and Electronic Computers.
However, the chapter will concentrate on the sub-segment Electronic Computers, here the case of smartphones. This for a simple reason: Smartphones already a part of our daily lives (cf. KeepCoding 2017).
The internet connectivity of smartphones in combination with connectivity capabilities of other devices makes their importance evident, at least from a theoretical perspective. The machine smartphone communicates with other machines to obtain, process and sends data, which in turn is transformed again by other devices. Knowledge workers use smartphones intensively exactly for these purposes, for work tasks but also for private matters and thus turned into highly relevant tools: In this research smartphone can be summarized as a device which helps the knowledge worker to get more information, which influences his decisions and consequential actions, even without the presence of strong AI.

In the future, strong AI will also be able to find its way into the smartphone industry, which is one of the largest manufacturing industries today. However, to what extent does strong AI is going to change the smartphone industry and what might be the significant changes in short-term?
Continuous efforts by companies such as Apple, Google, Huawei, Samsung, and others gave birth to smartphone AI technology. Current use-cases of machine learning and AI in smartphones are features such as voice-to-text translation, existing AI agents like Apple's Siri, Google Assistant or common applications like Apple or Google Maps. These features and many more will expand across the industry, complemented

by embedded AI in all parts of mobile devices from cameras, to audio, to machine (cf. Fuertes 2017; Narula 2018).

Emerging tech based on AI now enables smartphones to learn and recognize their users. In general, many predictions say that AI will transform phones to their next iteration, because unusually deep learning algorithms or neural networks, which recognizes sensory patterns as they happen. It is the reason image recognition, speech transcription, and translation have become more accurate. Upcoming capabilities in the field of strong AI will bring a further shift in technology and could fundamentally change the smartphone in the future. For example, Huawei's consumer head of software and intelligence engineering said (cf. Reichert 2017; Fuertes 2017; Morrissey 2017; Coughlin 2017):

> "If you look at the whole ecosystem, the AI will fundamentally change the phone from the smartphone to the intelligent phone" (Reichert 2017).

Considering today's so-called AI applications in smartphones, at the core they are using machine learning and in detail a convolutional neural network, which is a type of weak AI and still many steps away from strong AI. The smartphones nowadays learn to recognize patterns from a significant amount of raw data, which usually takes place on massive server farms because it requires an immense amount of data. A machine learning application can then apply the patterns trained or learned in the first step to more data. For a smartphone, the latter step is most relevant. A trained neural network is already used for example to recognize objects or faces in an image (cf. Herget 2018). As mentioned above, current devices that run AI algorithms depend on servers in the cloud, because the device itself lacks the horsepower to run AI algorithms. Using these servers limits how information is processed and is only working with online connectivity by sending data back and forth.
A so-called on-device AI unit could change that process and increase the computing power of the device itself. It describes a processor dedicated to machine learning for mobile phones and other smart-home devices. This might be the most significant changes in the global smartphone market soon by climbing the way to strong AI. AI smartphones could be standard in the future by putting this chip in every single mobile device. It seems very attractive because could speed things up, cutting the lag inherent in sending information back and forth. It will allow hardware to run offline, which pleases privacy advocates, who are comforted by the idea of data remaining on the device (cf. Rahman 2018; Condliffe 2018).

Instead of always sharing data with a company server, AI can analyze the user's data on-device, which keeps it personal and under the user's control. In addition to this possibly better data protection, it could also improve the battery performance of the devices, as a consequence of data being processed and stored locally (cf. Lomas 2018; Coughlin 2017).

> "It's also predicting that, by 2022, a full 80 percent of smartphones shipped will have on-device AI capabilities, up from just 10 percent in 2017." (Lomas 2018).

A few smartphones already have their on-device AI or also called the neural processing unit, which according to manufacturers is meant to make smartphones smart. In modern smartphones, it mainly includes functions related to image recognition, photography or processing (cf. Herget 2018).

Primarily these upcoming AI chips can digest massive data sets based on the user's habits, daily patterns, and past behaviors. This current type of AI can retrieve supporting information from mobile apps, fitness trackers, digital watches, or even browsing history. The goal is to make predictions about what the user might do next. In the future, a standard on-device AI for smartphones coming closer to strong AI and could make it possible, as mentioned above, that all analysis will be able to take place on a device without an internet connection, which is a revolutionary thought (cf. Coughlin 2017). Furthermore, this on device AI will change two key aspects of the smartphone shortly. On the one hand user-machine interaction, and on the other hand context-personalized openness. The first aspect will improve efficiencies between the user and his phone across text, image, voice, video, and sensors, while the second will actively provide services and aggregated information across apps, content, third-party features, and essential features (cf. Reichert 2017). It could be imaginable that strong AI might be the highest level of smartphones for everything in the daily life of the future.

However, there are many other benefits of AI in smartphones. For example, emotion sensing systems (emotion recognition) and affective computing will lead to an increase in personal assistance, which means better context and enhanced service experience. It will allow smartphones to detect, analyze, process and respond to his user's emotions and moods. It could also understand the user's interests and tastes, even prioritizing notifications, more accurately. An apparent product of smartphone AI also enables devices to give predictions on how we can improve our lives. By that, a health app could scan the user's body, pull readings from phone sensors, and determine if anything is unbalanced. In that case, users could be notified immediately. A few scholars estimate that soon the smartphone might be able to detect precursors for illnesses such as cardiovascular diseases, Parkinson's or dementia. Even car manufacturers could use a smartphones front camera to understand the physical conditions of drivers or gauge fatigue levels to increase safety. Other benefits are for business people, who are always multitasking, an improved AI phone can de-clutter their calendar, schedule their conference calls, even record and transcribe notes from a presentation. It could also boost battery life, charge faster or increase storage space. Unless consumer spending on mobile phones and apps slows down expect to see, these features rolled out in the future. Continuous training and deep learning on smartphones will also improve the accuracy of natural-language understanding (speech recognition), while better understanding the user's specific intentions. The last promising application for AI might be augmented reality, where digital effects provide an additional visual layer on top of the camera or captured image. All in all the most noticeable changes AI will bring are processing speed, efficiency and new paths of opportunities (cf. Coughlin 2017; Lomas 2018; Fuertes 2017).

Especially regarding the characteristics of strong AI in chapter two, its use-cases in smartphones are still very young but poised to have a transformational impact on the mobile device of the future. It will create a personalized, more and more user-friendly and beneficial relationship between the smartphone and its user. The smartphone is on the way of being a perfect personal assistant for everyday use of the consumer even for information worker because strong AI will bring smartphones to a much higher level in the future.

5.4. Media of Communication

The preceding analysis has shown the potential for signification effects of strong AI on industry segments. It may be assumed that this will also be the case for the segment Media of Communication. Changes in ICT will profoundly impact today's media structures, the media industry will change too. Substantial amounts of goods produced by the media industry can be digitalized. The internet and mobile devices are an ideal means to distribute digitilized goods. Consequently, the media communication and distribution of content shifts from traditional media like papers, magazines and books and outlet selling these goods to internet-enabled devices such as the smartphone (cf. Dolata/ Schrape 2012: 7).

One goal of this chapter is to explore current and near-future use cases of AI in Media of Communication. Using the approach again to dwell deeper into sub-segments of an industry, the chapter looks at the sub-segments advertising and broadcasting. Other communications based on smartphone apps, social media, email, online chat rooms or communication with chatbots are not being investigated. So all the applications, cited in the following chapter will by no means be exhaustive or definitive for the Media and communication as a whole. However, the selected sub-segment may still help to find insights into the validity of the two stated hypotheses: the impact of strong AI on job availability and knowledge workers in the Media of Communication Industry.
Before starting the analysis, a closer definition of the industry shall be applied. The Media of Communication cover as well as oral communication media as written communication media. In detail oral communication describes the process of communication in which messages or information is exchanged or communicated within sender and receiver through word of mouth. It can be sub-divided into speaking and listening. Written communication includes messages or information, which is exchanged or communicated within sender and receiver through written form, so writing or reading (cf. The Business Communication 2018).

The first analyzes object will be the advertising sector. At first glance, it can be seen that digital advertising and media might be very suitable playgrounds for strong AI. The already used applications of AI in advertising and its connected media are as varied as they are numerous, ranging from ad targeting, content curation, and creation, or dynamic pricing, through fraud prevention, predictive customer service and product recommendation, to programmatic buying, sales forecasting, and web or app personalization. Through the combination of different technologies based on AI, consumer experience could be brought to the next level. The fact is that humans are simply not able to analyze and interpret all available data that can be gleaned from consumer habits. Sure, they can spot patterns and act accordingly, but this is incredibly inefficient when compared to what the current level of AI can already do and what especially strong AI could do in the future. Strong AI and machine learning algorithms can leverage billions of data points to make predictions for future campaigns, and then use real-time information to optimize throughout. The following scenario could picture one promising implementation of AI in advertising, based on the assumption that a fashion style of person gives information about its buying behavior: A customer enters a store where an image recognition system identifies her fashion style for example. The profile is then fed into a second system that uses the preferences of consumers with similar styles to recommend specific products or colors, or else to deliver the most suitable content via in-store displays (cf. Maugain 2017, Fritschle 2017). In this sense, strong AI in advertising could mean new uncovered opportunities for brands, customer enhancement by understanding their behavior in marketing or an appropriate targeting of advertising in a sense, bringing up the right information, at the right time, through the right channel.

The second analyze object is broadcasting. Compared to other industries, there seem to be fewer articles that focus on AIs application to broadcast, or how it delivers unquestionable and immediately realizable benefits. However, it is not easy to determine which segments of the broadcast or even its connected media industry get the most significant impact from developments in AI. Based on the qualitative analysis for this research, it can be argued that broadcast can take advantage of strong AI by providing new opportunities for helping to enhance metadata and provide closed captioning. Ethan Dreilinger (IBM Watson, solutions engineer) said one of its main early beachheads is in diving into broadcasters extensive archives and cleaning up its metadata to improve retrievability, along with real-time closed captioning services. Furthermore, there might also be the promise image recognition for audience analysis as a potential mainstream application. On content, recognizing images from live or recorded videos could lead to metadata tags or descriptive information of a movie or a program beyond its usual essential attributes such as genre, language or actors. Due to the potential of strong AI, it is also starting to learn the roles of an editor or creative director for television commercials and may soon help suss out fake news. Concerning more general use cases for AI in content creation and delivery, the two most viewer-centric applications would be on content discovery and content personalization. Its primary goal is to deliver personalized and targeted experiences to multiscreen audiences to keep them coming back. Furthermore the same applies to ad targeting because advertisements can also be tailored to the audience - based on their demographics or preferences.

All the applications cited in this chapter are by no means exhaustive or definitive. However, it seems evident, that we will see growing adoption of AI-powered solutions in different aspects of broadcasting. For example from enhancing metadata, providing closed captioning or content creation to management, delivery, or consumption (cf. Fronda 2017, Depp 2018; Lant 2017).

Based on the elaboration on the Media of Communication, it may be concluded – as for the other investigated industries – that profound changes arising from strong AI have to be expected for the entire industry, even only a sub-segment has been investigated here.

5.5. Research and Development

Machlup describes research and development as a sub-segment, which combines two knowledge-producing activities. On the one hand, new knowledge about how things are or how things could be made is originated in the mind of the researcher, discoverer, inventor, or developer. On the other hand, this knowledge is also produced in the minds of others. In the first part of the chapter research and development should be defined more precisely. Regarding research, it has become customary to distinguish between basic and applied research work. The general idea behind the distinction between basic and applied research is that basic research creates basic knowledge, on which practical, applicable knowledge may rest but which itself is too general, too broad or too deep, to have direct applications. In contrast, applied research creates directly applicable knowledge. So the main difference is while in basic research the investigator looks for general laws, with no regard to practical use, in applied research he looks for results which promise to be of ultimate use in practice. For example, the better understanding of the physical or organic world is the goal of the basic research, better products or better ways of making them are the goals of the applied research. It sounds like a rather clear contrast between the two types of work, but in reality, the borderline cases are very numerous.
Even more difficult than the distinction between basic and applied research is the separation between research and development. Not only the question of where development starts is hard to answer, also the question of where it ends is equally troublesome (cf. Machlup 1962: 145 ff.). So there might be many complex and intertwined distinctions, not feasible to handle in this chapter. Against that backdrop, there should be no specific focus on research or development.

All in all, there are very fewer starting points for strong AI in both fields anyway. One reason might be that as well research as development is too abstract and complicated for being done by AI-driven resources. Human skills such as multidimensional thinking, recognizing structures or creativity are essential. Regarding the current state of the art strong AI seems very far away to disrupt the fields of research and development.

Compared to the already analyzed industries of the information economy there are also almost no qualitative data, makes it hard to discuss possible use-cases of strong AI in the future within this field. So the following paragraph might be more theoretical what could be changed within this sub-segment.
However, it seems interesting to note that applications could arise within this field that focuses on the cooperation between scientists and machines. Both regarding knowledge acquisition, as well as in the evaluation of large data sets, a virtual scientist based on strong AI could be imaginable. In the long run, for example, it would be conceivable that scientists must not collect data themselves. By that, they would focus on more complex tasks, which could only be done by a human scientist. Intending to development, AI could take over a part of control tasks for the goal realizations in the form of an omniscient virtual guide in real time. Even tasks such as feedback and risk assessment in advance of a planned development project would be conceivable.

In summary, there are clear limits to the impact of strong AI in this area. Based on the qualitative Analysis there are no scientific contributions yet how to revolutionize this field with strong AI.

6. Interim Conclusion and Hypotheses

6.1. Evaluation of the First Analysis

The previous analysis of sub-segments of the information economy according to Machlup's framework has delivered various indications, that strong AI will have a profound impact on the information economy and information society. The currently present scope of AI has already produced changes. While supporting the notion that AI increases efficiency and productivity. Considering the analyzed potential of strong AI, it can be further well argued that AI can replace human labor. However, it is uncertain to determine yet that labor replacement takes place "only" in the form of human-machine interaction or by a more complete takeover of AI, substituting human work activity even too much higher degree. The industry sector analysis was undertaken in the previous chapter rather points to the human-machine scenario.
In a comparison of the individual case studies, it is also to be assumed that more digitized areas such as financial services will be affected more

quickly by strong AI than less digitized ones like education sector. In consequence, digitalization is a basis for strong AI.
Returning to the hypotheses stipulated in chapter three applied to the subsequent analysis, the following conclusion may be allowed.

(a) The occupational structures resulting from todays information societies will be affected by massive labor market changes due to strong AI. As a consequence, AI has the potential to disrupt the main subdivisions of the information economy.

Changes will be deep and profound in many areas of the Information Economy. Efficiency gains resulting from strong AI will be strong. Even so strong that many human jobs, will become obsolete or only carried out in different ways and in conjunction with AI. The trend will first only apply to rather simpler tasks but will also later extend to more and more complex jobs. The changes to the job structures of information societies already occurring as described in chapter three will continue. On the labor market, demand will shift to ever higher and differently qualified employees, the lower skilled workforce will be at the detriment.
In addition, it could also be argued that Strong AI would mean that no longer only people are competing for a particular job with each other, but also the AI system with people. By that, even the highest skilled knowledge worker could end up with machines doing their jobs.

So, in both cases, the effect on occupation structures within the information economy will be, and the first thesis can be confirmed by the analysis so far. However, as a limitation of the analysis, it needs to be stated, that only a few sectors of the information economy have been looked at. Further research may confirm the conclusions made here but could also show different conflicting outcomes.
The second hypothesis relates to the potential advantages of strong AI:

(b) The beginning of strong AI seems to be the key for the information society to work more efficiently with the upcoming almost unmeasurable amounts of data and their complexity. AI can perform better than every single knowledge worker could do. As a consequence, the disruptive impact of strong AI will change the concept of knowledge workers as well as their relevance as their range of tasks within the Information Economy.

Based on the analysis undertaken on industry segments in chapter five, it can also be assumed that AI leads to higher productivity. Information workers used AI as an ICT product, processing higher amounts of data more efficiently.
However, the extent to which this might materialize, in particular for strong AI yielding more results and higher productivity as a knowledge worker can achieve, is strongly subject to the degree of complexity of individual jobs in and across industry segments. Further investigations are required here. Nevertheless, considering the results of the case studies, it can be hardly disputed that AI will be increasingly deployed, thus resulting in profound changes on the required skills sets for knowledge workers as well as changing the ways and means to do their jobs.

As illustrated in chapter three, Drucker sees his productivity as the most valuable asset in the 21st century. Considering time frames, in a first wave of AI deployment, the productivity of information workers will be increased using intelligent systems and applications in the form of human-machine interaction. The use of smartphones connected to devices and machines to process data and generate transactions is only on the example here. In a second wave, strong AI could even substitute knowledge workers by providing better efficiency and productivity as a knowledge worker could achieve.

6.2. Hypotheses for the Second Analysis

The previous case studies of the information economy after Machlup have shown that substantial effects of AI deployment can be expected in at least four of the five sub-industry segments analyzed. This gives rise to the following questions: What will happen on a macro level if strong AI more or less simultaneously and equally effects all micro-levels? Are actions to countervail effects of AI on societal, political or governmental levels required? And if so, which actions might produce which required results?
To attempt to answer these questions, the dimension of AI impacts on the macro-level shall be discussed using the following hypothesis:

(a) Strong AI can mean the erosion of today's information economy by affecting employment in the way that it will destroy more jobs than creating new ones for the same educated workforce.

This Thesis is developed by the results of the analysis of the Information Economy. Since the impact of strong AI on the Information Economy is so massive, the following chapter will seek to establish further the validity of the action claim put forward by looking at already occurring impacts of AI. These short elaborations seek to foster the rather theoretical argument to Machlup's framework with current evidence. After these supposed consequences of strong AI have been set out, it should be concentrated on the investigation of another hypothesis:

(b) To encounter the highly likely effects of AI and in particular strong AI, governments should seek actions to shape the effects of technological changes on the society and facilitate more equal distribution of the positive effects of technical changes.

The question here then is, what should governments and even whole societies should actually do, which strategies shall be implemented, which actions taken? The discussion on the two hypotheses formulated above shall take place in the next two chapters.

7. Supposed Consequences of AI

Based on the analysis of the information economy (see Chapter 5), it can be assumed that strong AI has the potential to disrupt the main subdivisions of the information economy and the occupational structures, which result from today's information societies and will be affected by massive labor market changes resulting from the use of strong AI. Also, the use of AI will result in profound changes in the required skills set for knowledge workers, as well as changing the ways and means to do their jobs. As mentioned in the last chapter, the following section will review the results of this analysis using recent studies and further literature.

The first challenge constitutes the fact that there are no isolated studies and statistics with a singular focus on strong AI. One reason for this may be that recent studies and the majority of the literature on AI, in contrast to this work, did not make differentiation of AI into weak and strong AI. Instead, AI is used as an umbrella term; severely limiting the precision of the analysis. In general, AI-driven automation is often covered by the same statistics as digitalization or computerization. Thus, it is not possible to show only strong AI within this chapter.

Because of the missing data on strong AI, and its possible impact on the economy, statistics on AI-driven automation and computerization are discussed as a relevant phenomenon in this chapter. Based on this it should be assumed that the impact of the ongoing digitalization on society will increase significantly and speed up with strong AI as an accelerator for these developments in the future.

Based on the further literature, the current state of AI is already becoming more deeply integrated into people's lives, and with further improvements towards strong AI in different industries, it could become the new infrastructure. It will further accelerate the often quoted ongoing industrial revolution (cf. Rotman 2017; Narula 2018; Wahlmüller-Schiller 2017). Especially when the analyzed potential of strong AI in the information economy comes true, a remarkable revolution will be ushered in. Due to the multifold impact of AI and the ongoing digitalization in the information economy, entire socio-economic systems of information societies already entered a phase of accelerating transformation. Consequently, markets, businesses, government, social welfare, education and employment models will be impacted severely more and more (cf. Krasadakis 2017). It is already predicted that the speed of technological change from the forthcoming AI revolution will rise sharply; opening significant opportunities for growth and profitability, as well as novel challenges and competition (cf. Makridakis 2017: 18).

Today, it may be challenging to predict exactly how the labor market will change and which jobs will be most immediately affected by AI-driven automation. As mentioned above, AI is not a single technology, but rather a collection of technologies that are applied to specific tasks. This means that the effects of AI will be felt unevenly across the economy. There will be work tasks more easily automated than others, and even there will be jobs, which will be more affected than others. However, based on the current trajectory of AI technology in general, some specific predictions are possible (cf. U.S. Government 2016: 8). AI and robotics are driving rapid and radical workplace transformation across all industries, for small and large companies (cf. EmTech 2018). In ten years, industries will not look anything like today, and in 20 years, much of today's jobs will no longer exist (cf. Braun 2015). The following illustration shows diverse industries that will be affected first:

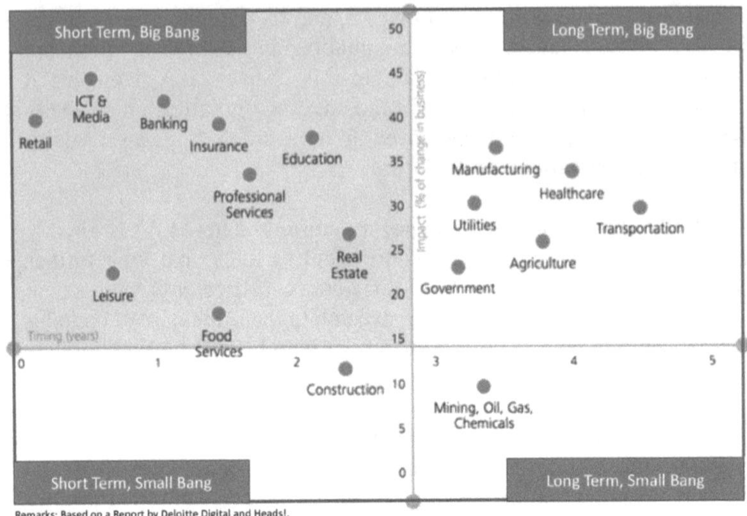

Figure VI: Industry Disruption Map. Similar: Deloitte Digital 2015: 1.

The illustration shows the impact of AI across different industry sectors. In the short- and mid-term, AI will significantly impact specific industries, such as retail, banking, insurance or education. However, in the long run, AI may have impacted almost every type of industry that exists today.

Nevertheless, based on the research so far, it can be assumed that more digitized areas will be affected by strong AI faster than less digitized ones. And the more complex the requirements within an industry are for certain tasks that require, for example, a high level of creativity, the later strong AI will exert influence. All in all, within these modern industries the world's top tech companies are in a race to build the best AI and capture that massive market means the technology will get better fast and increase its impact on society at all (cf. Maney 2016).

> "There is little doubt that AI holds enormous potential as computers and robots will probably achieve, or come close to, human intelligence over the next twenty years becoming a serious competitor to all the jobs currently performed by humans and for the first time raising doubt over the end of human supremacy." (Makridakis 2017: 2)

Based on the literature on AI and computerization, as well as its potential impact on the future work dynamics, many studies are looking at expected job losses in the near future. The following table shows an overview of some of the different related studies between 2013 and 2017:

Authors:	Country/ Region	Jobs at risk in percent (%)	Based on Frey/ Osborne	Own research
Frey/ Osborne (2013) [1]	USA	47		X
Bowles (2014) [2]	EU	46-62	X	
De Jong et al. (2014) [3]	Netherland	24	X	
Ekeland et al. (2015) [4]	Finnland, Norway	33	X	
Brzeski et al. (2015) [5]	Germany	59	X	
Bonin et al. (2015) [6]	Germany	42	X	
Arntz et al. (2016) [7]	OECD	6-9	X	
World Bank (2016) [8]	World	37-83	X	
Chang/ Huynh (2016) [9]	ASEAN-5	44-70	X	
World Economic Forum (2016) [10]	15 countries	-		X
Manyika et al. (2017) [11]	46 countries	5+		X
Bührer et al. (2017) [12]	Germany	46	X	

[1] **Frey/ Osborne (2013)**: The Future of Employment: How Susceptible are Jobs to Computerization?, University Oxford; [2] **Bowles 2014**: Chart of the Week: 54% of EU jobs at risk of computerization, Brügel, Blog Post, online: http://bruegel.org/2014/07/chart-of-the-week-54-of-eu-jobs-at-risk-of- computerisation/; [3] **De Jon et al. (2014)**: De impact van automatisering op de Nederlandse Arbeidsmarkt. Een gedegen verkenning op basis van Data Analystics, Deloitte Research, Amstelveen; [4] **Ekeland et al. (2015)**: Computerization threatens one-third of Finnish and Norwegian Employment, ETLA Briefs, 22. Research Institute of the Finnish Economy, Helsinki; [5] **Brzeski et al. (2015)**: Die Roboter kommen. Folgen der Automatisierung für den deutschen Arbeitsmarkt, ING DiBa Research, Frankfurt a.M; [6] **Bonin at al. (2015)**: Übertragung der Studie von Frey/Osborne (2013) auf Deutschland, ZEW Kurzexpertise, Nr. 57, Mannheim; [7] **Arntz et al. (2016)**: The Risk of Automation for Jobs in OECD Countries: A Comparative Analysis, OECD Social, Employment and Migration Working Papers, Nr. 189, OECD Publishing, Paris 2016; [8] **World Bank (2016)**: World Development Report 2016, Washington DC; [9] **Chang/ Huynh (2016)**: ASEAN in Transformation. The Future of Jobs at Risk of Automation, International Labour Organisation Regional Office for Asia and the Pacific Working Paper, Nr. 9, Genf; [10] **World Economic Forum (2016)**: The Future of Jobs: Employment, Skills and Workforce Strategy for the Fourth Industrial Revolution; [11] **Manyika et al. (2017):** A future that works: automation, employment, and productivity, McKinsey Global Institute; [12] **Bührer et al. (2017):** The Effect of Digitalization on the Labor Market, in: H. Ellermann; P. Kreutter, W. Messner (Hrsg.): The Palgrave Handbook of Managing Continuous Business Transformation, München. (similar: **Heinen et al. 2017**).

As shown in the table, Frey and Osbornes (2013) are frequently quoted and their research paper from Oxford University "The future of employment" particularly, is a widely used research basis for other scholars. For this reason, this chapter will focus on the future of employment mostly based on the assumptions of Fred and Osborne's. The consequences that will be addressed in the chapter are decisive for the further course of this research. They summarize the theoretical stance of the researcher assume that massive job losses become a problem in the future.

> "Technology has always changed employment, but the rise of robotics and artificial intelligence could transform it beyond recognition" (Oxford University 2016).

Frey and Osbornes proclaimed that AI and robots will replace approximately 47 percent of all US jobs over the next ten to twenty years (cf. Frey/ Osborne 2013: 38; Hummert et al. 2018). That is one result of their study, which examined more than 700 detailed forms of occupation, noting the types of tasks workers performed and the skills required. By weighting these chosen factors, as well as the engineering obstacles currently preventing computerization, they assessed the degree to which these occupations may be automated in the near future. Particularly, the availability of big data was identified as one major trend that is given engineers a large dataset to work with. This has made it possible for computers to deal with problems that, until recently, only people could handle. The job cuts will be forced by robots and AI (cf. Dirican 2015; Sandhana 2013).

Both also believe that these job losses will occur in two stages and are not limited to neither unskilled labor jobs nor blue-collar trades (cf. Oxford University 2018; Lant 2017b). In the first stage, computers will start replacing people in especially vulnerable fields like transportation or logistics, production labor, and administrative support. Furthermore, jobs in sales, services or construction will too be lost. By the end of the first stage, they proclaim that the rate of replacement will slow down due to bottlenecks in harder-to-automate fields such as engineering. The first stage will be followed by a second stage, which includes another wave of computerization, dependent upon the development of strong artificial intelligence. This second stage could put more complex jobs for example in management, science and engineering, and the arts at risk (cf. Rutkin 2013).

> "Our findings thus imply that as technology races ahead, low-skill workers will reallocate to tasks that are non- susceptible to computerization – i.e., tasks requiring creative and social intelligence. For workers to win the race, however, they will have to acquire creative and social skills." (Sandhana 2013).

Frey and Osborne further argue that jobs that require social intelligence, creativity or cognition and fine motor skills will be among those activities that better secure against disruption of AI or robots. It is expected that occupations with these job profiles will become more important (cf. Eichhorst et al., 2015; U.S. Government 2016; Mahdawi 2017). So acquiring more creative and social skills coupled with higher education level seems necessary, as high-skill jobs are less likely to be replaced anytime soon.

Many other experts have confirmed the main results of these studies. Economist of Harvard University, Larry Summers, for example, warns of the threat of massive job losses, whereby he warrants attention to the issue that there may be more industries that lose jobs than industries that create jobs (cf. Turner 2014). Furthermore, the World Economic Forum estimated that 65 percent of children entering primary schools now grow up to work in jobs that do not yet exist (cf. Macmillen 2017). Erik Brynjolfsson and Andrew McAfee from the Massachusetts Institute of Technology sum up this development in their book "The Second Machine Age" in 2014. They underline the high risk of massive job cuts and the mass-unemployment as a transitional phenomenon as inevitable (cf. Brynjolfsson et al. 2014). From today's point of view, even a part of the new IT jobs introduced by digitization could be directly replaced by AI anytime soon. In conclusion, every technological transformation destroys jobs, but also creates new ones. Yet, AI-driven automaton will be the first transformation that destroys more jobs than it will create new one.

However, this rather pessimistic future scenario is also opposed by optimists who believe that AI-driven automation will not cause massive job losses.

> "Some optimists argue that AI is no different than technologies that came before it and that centuries of fears that machines will replace human labor have proven unfounded, with machines instead creating previously unimagined jobs and raising incomes." (Furman 2016).

This argument is taken up again in the critical review (see Chapter 9) of this work but should not be considered in the context of further work. In the following course of this research, it should be assumed that the worse scenario describes the mass unemployment as a conceivable future scenario.

Due to AI-driven automation, also socio-economic inequality may increase sharply. Several scholars claim that even if technological automation may not increase unemployment, it can destroy middle-range jobs while increasing those on the low and high ends, augmenting social inequality as the pay between low and high-end jobs is amplified (cf. Makridakis 2017: 19ff.; Maney 2016; Brynjolfsson et al. 2014; O´Neil 2016). Therefore, the focus should evolve more around the question of how much people will get paid if they will lose their jobs (cf. Kletzer

2018). As an interim result, possible future scenarios characterized by mass unemployment or even strong social-economic inequalities can be summarized.
Nevertheless, there is uncertainty about these possible socio-economic consequences of AI, regarding exactly when and how they will occur in the future. According to Bill Gates talking about technology:

> "We always overestimate the change that will occur in the next two years and underestimate the change that will occur in the next 10." (Wray 2017).

Moreover, AI is a non-linear, tightly coupled and an astonishing technology, which makes its future even harder to predict (cf. D´Monte 2018; Metz 2018; Dempsey 2017). However, based on the research so far: Strong AI will change the information society including its economy and landscape of work. There is a consensus in the literature that AI will change the way humans work. The question is when and in which manner this change happen.

Overall, based on the concept of the information society and the analysis of the information economy, two possible scenarios should be considered further. Based on this, political options and possible policy outcomes will be discussed in the next chapter.
The first scenario is oriented on the short- and mid-term: "Increasing human-machine integration and transformation". The second one is more oriented on the mid- and long-term: "Idle human resources, further caused by a huge skill gap - even the highest skilled knowledge worker could end up with machines; discussing massive unemployment and rising inequality.

7.1. Short- Midterm Szenario: Increasing Human-Machine Integration and Transformation

All in all, based on previous research, an increasing human-machine integration can be observed in most industries of the information economy. Furthermore, it is assumed that this integration will continue to increase and become deeper than ever. As mentioned above, this human-machine collaboration can go many different ways; constituting a great potential for the entire information economy. The following chapter will briefly describe this expected human-machine symbiosis.

The rise of AI already presents a shifting division of work between humans and machines. The goal is to bring their different strengths together. This means every part could concentrate on individual tasks performed best by each party, respectively. For example, on the one hand, humans are good at creative thinking, problem-solving, conversations, generalization, and abstraction. On the other hand, machines are better for accessing databases, performing repetitive tasks, mathematical calculations and lifting heavy objects. So, by concentrating on their individual strengths, a human-machine collaboration can be very useful, which has already shown to lead to increased efficiency in the economy. Regarding the process of decision making, for instance, the partnership between human decision makers and AI can play out in two ways: First, humans and AI technologies can collaborate to deal with different aspects of decision-making. AI is likely to be well positioned to tackle complexity issues by using analytical approaches. This allows humans to focus more on uncertainty and equivocality, using more creative and intuitive approaches. Second, even the most complex decisions, in which AI has a competitive edge, are likely to entail elements of equivocality and uncertainty. Therefore, humans continue to play an important role in almost all complex situations, as do AI in the face of equivocality and uncertainty.

Against this background, collaboration between humans and AI in a decision-making situation can be illustrated using the following graphic based on complexity, ambiguity and uncertainty:

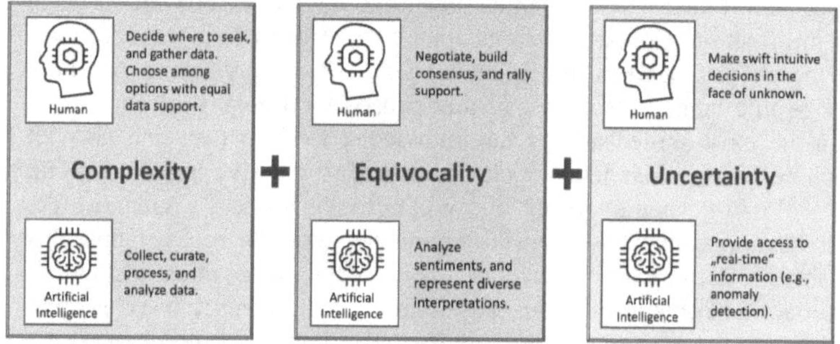

Figure VII: Human-AI Collaboration in decision-making. Source: Own graphic, similar: Jarrahi 2018.

The graphic shows that the pervasive visions of a partnership between humans and machines suggest that machines should take care of less creative mundane tasks, allowing humans to focus on more abstract work (cf. Jarrahi 2018: 9f.). In practice, this could work in a very simple way, without consuming too much time or extra work. For example, each firm could bring an AI software in their conference room. Then the AI should be able to listen to the conversation in a business meeting while continually searching the internet for information that might be relevant, then serve it up when asked. So, it could support with knowledge of the outside world that the humans might not be aware of, which will lead to better decisions. By use-cases like this, scholars already believe that artificial intelligence will also improve human intelligence (cf. Maney 2016; Carter et al. 2018). Human-Machine Symbiosis in decision-making is just one example of describing benefits from human-machine collaboration.

All in all, based on the previous research a partnership like this can be expected, even if human intelligence and machine intelligence comprise an entirely different nature. The pattern recognition capabilities of big data and deep learning algorithms will assist humans to make new discoveries if yet requiring human intelligence to guide the AI devices as to what patterns to look for (cf. Braga 2017: 2f.).

7.2. Mid- Longterm Szenario: Discussing e.g. Massive Unemployment, Inequality and other Security Issues

Based on the first part of chapter seven and the analysis of strong AI in the information economy (See Chapter 5) a mid- to long-term scenario can be characterized in the following way: Caused by strong AI, there will be idle human resources, further caused by a huge skill gap. Thus, even the most skilled among the knowledge workers may end up with machines doing their job, which could lead to massive unemployment. Regardless of whether or not this will actually happen, a scenario like this seems possible based on the conducted research so far. Thus, this pessimistic scenario could involve raising social and political instability, lost identity, crime or other security issues, which seems to be relevant to describe in the first part of this chapter. The impact of this scenario on the political macro-level and societies will be described in the last part of this chapter. It is assumed that its major challenges for today's information societies can be expected. The negative potential of mass unemployment could massively influence the central functions of today's information societies. Starting with the development of job cuts, which in effect leads to less purchasing power of citizens and thus reduction of

demand. Also, the concept of traditional wage labor and workers unions erodes and remains at most only for a small part of the population. Without work, on an individual level, many citizens could lose their identity or even suffer psychological problems because they always were used to work. All these aspects could trigger a change in values or even a loss of confidence in the state. Looking back at history, it can be learned that especially times of value changes, whether through technological innovations or external aggressors, are troubled times for all kinds of relationships within a society.
These upheavals are also accompanied by problems that come to the state, for example, lower tax revenues for the state as fewer people work, but rising expenditure caused by social measures, such as unemployment benefits, will inevitably lead to massive financial gaps in the state. How can a state help compensate for the needs of the unemployed people to pay for their living if they have no money for that? Answering and investigating such a question might be beyond the scope of this chapter, but serious problems based on this scenario seem realistic. Especially when the negative effects increase and the needs of the citizens, such as work or equal compensation, to maintain their standard of living is not met, this leads to serious threats to politics and society.

Social or political instability, lost identity, poverty, riots, populism, crime or other security issues can potentially also be seen as a by-product of developments in rising unemployment. This raises the following questions: How many unemployed or social inequalities the information society can tolerate in the long run and when it collapses? Are existing societies prepared for, or able to cope with, the challenges of increasing levels of strong AI, and thus possible increases in unemployment? If the pessimistic line of this chapter is continued, for example, today's capitalism in its current form would no longer be conceivable. An increasing number of scientists are addressing the issue of rethinking today's social and economic systems and the development of alternative systems. More commonly accompanying terms are: „The end of capitalism has begun“, “radical new economic system of the future“, „postcapitalism“ or even „decline of democracies“. All these scholars recommend, that governments have to reinvent existing economies and societies to keep up with accelerating technology (cf. Brynjolfsson et al: 2014; Confino 2014; Mason 2015; Helbing et al. 2017). „It’s time to start discussing what kind of society we should construct around a labor- light economy. How should the abundance of such an economy be shared? How can the tendency of modern capitalism to produce high levels of inequality be muted while preserving its ability to allocate resources efficiently and reward initiative and effort? What do fulfilling lives and healthy communities look like when they no longer center on industrial-era conceptions of work?" (Makridakis 2017: 20f.).

Yet, before turning to these questions, the analysis throughout of the current paper suggests the need to create political strategies to avoid scenarios of increasing mass unemployment or social inequality.

8. Different Models of Political Reactions

The outlined AI revolution and emerging trends in IT will unfold over the coming decades with enormous opportunities, challenges, and implications for the information society.

> "To harness these benefits, countries will need to create conditions that support the deployment of next-generation networks and service infrastructures. In order to track the growth and impact of these emerging ICT trends, new global indicators will need to be put in place." (International Telecommunication Union 2017).

Thus, policy makers need to invent ways to make sure that everyone in society benefits because they have a responsibility to support the positive future development of their respective countries. Questions raised on a political macro-level are for example: How do regulators make these new patterns in AI and humanity symbiotic? How do politicians interact with emerging tech and new opportunities offered by AI?
Regulators, politicians, and policy makers are called upon to create conditions facilitating entrepreneurial experiments and innovation, and to find out how a human-machine integration can work most efficiently. Policies will also have to mitigate challenges to employment, rising inequality but also information security and privacy issues (cf. Rotman 2017; International Telecommunication Union 2017).

All in all, many political questions are coming up and should be answered before it is too late, and the pessimistic scenario outlined in chapter eight comes true. Politicians should support and invest in research about all relevant topics such as privacy, ethical and social issues as well as new concepts for the future world of work. International efforts are getting more important to work on these global topics caused by AI. Establishing a cross-cultural dialogue about specific AI issues and building a learning network for investigating approaches to address these issues within and across domestic and global contexts, are an important outcome (cf. Berkman Klein Center 2017), as exemplified by the first US-China AI summit in June 2018 in California, Monterey.

The most important goal should be that the negative consequences should be mitigated or made compatible with society. In the following, approaches to possible policy reactions are discussed in response to both scenarios developed in chapter eight.

8.1. Retraining, Focus on Education and Prepare a New Workforce

As already discussed in chapter seven, scholars believe that AI will bring innovations that will change the way people work and the skills demanded by the labor market. However, the technological upheaval will cause disruption. For example, a recent survey commissioned by Northeastern University in Massachusetts and conducted by Gallup finds that most of the American workers believe they are ill-prepared to deal with AI's expected impact on the global digital economy (cf. Northeastern News 2018). Policy makers have to make sure that people will get enough education, training, and support to even prepare for newly created jobs because of the technological upheaval. Because of this, funding in education and retraining programs focused on developing fusion skills for the age of AI can be one of the most important steps in the face of an increasing human-machine integration (cf. Dugherty/ Wilson 2018; Wachtel 2018). IT professor Acemoglu announced recently at MIT Technology Review's EmTech Next conference the central message:

> "Societies must invest in education and welfare services in order to realize the full benefits of robotics and AI. It's not anyone's responsibility by themselves; it's our collective responsibility." (Acemoglu MIT 2018).

A commitment to preparing citizens to adapt to continuous and rapid technological change, and the beginning of strong AI, requires pursuing policy changes that would significantly expand the availability of high-quality job training to meet the scale of need. In addition, regulators have to navigate job transitions of the people more successfully. Another key action towards preparing individuals for the economy of the future is providing quality education and specific training opportunities for all. By

that, it also gets increasingly important that governments make key investments in school education for children from all income backgrounds off to the right start (cf. U.S. Government 2016).
One conclusion of the first analysis of the information economy says that AI will aid humans to make better decisions in almost every industry. But to harness these benefits, each algorithm needs to be tailored carefully to existing data, and the objectives pursued, which requires considerable human expertise in machine learning and large datasets to train these algorithms (cf. International Telecommunication Union 2017). For this goal even information worker needs to be educated enough as well, so retraining-programs and basic research seems more important than ever for today's information societies. For example, based on the analysis of the information economy, within the education sector is an enormous potential for AI in the future. It is enabling teachers and students enormous benefits (See Chapter 5.1). But implementing and deploying this technology at school requires government investment in education resources.

All in all, governments and regulators also play an essential role in advancing the AI field by investing in basic research and development. They need to retrain the worker within the society and educate a workforce that develops AI, which includes researchers who drive fundamental advances in AI and related fields, a larger number of specialists who refine AI methods for specific applications, and a significant number of users who operate those applications in specific settings.
These workers of the future will also need comprehensive training in ethics. It is fundamental for them to navigate a world in which the value of human beings can no longer be taken for granted. Even the fields of cyberdefense and fraud detection are getting more and more important regarding the safety of the information society. But fundamental questions have to be answered still, like, can robots and humans work together just as smoothly? That is a current goal of researchers in the Tellex lab for example. They are trying to give both robots and humans the tools to understand each other a little better and work together more fluidly in real environments by understanding each other's different strengths and using them together in the most efficient way (cf. Regalado 2018; U.S. Government 2016: 27ff.; Mahroum 2018). This increasing human and machine integration could lead to a much better output of almost every kind of task. These technological benefits are a huge chance to solve the most important problems in an increasingly complex information society.

Against this background, education must be ensured and focused more than ever before. Especially based on the assumption that the demands on the jobs of the future will increase. Joseph E. Aoun, President of the Northeastern University in Massachusetts, recommends:

> "The answer to greater artificial intelligence is greater human intelligence." (Northeastern News 2018).

In conclusion, these education and retraining programs are important strategies for the future of today's information societies, in which the human-machine symbiosis will be essential. For this, it is essential to determine how people can work together in an optimal relationship with robots and AI-driven applications. This suggests that both humans and machines should better understand the opposing part. All in all the synthesis of tasks getting done by machines and others by people will be even smarter than just one side of the equation.

8.2. Discourse of a Basic Income

Whether strong AI causes a scenario of mass unemployment and increasing social inequality depends not only on the technology itself but also on the framework conditions of society, like institutions or policies, that are in place. On the basis of the literature dealing with the prevention of such future scenarios, some scholars believe the governments should institute a so-called basic income.

Especially as described in chapter eight, tech titans like Elon Musk or Bill Gates and the academics around them are concerned that AI and robots they have built will rapidly displace humans in the workforce, or at least push them into jobs with no room for growth (cf. Ito 2018; Freedman 2016; Amadeo 2018).
In summer 2016, former American president Obama addressed the idea of a universal basic income in an interview with the Director of MIT's Media Lab, Joi Ito:

> "Whether a universal income is the right model — is it gonna be accepted by a broad base of people? — that's a debate that we'll be having over the next 10 or 20 years." (Clifford 2016).

Against this backdrop, the basic-income concept has regained popularity. The idea is still mostly theoretical, but in the last years, there have been intensified discussions, concrete plans, and a number of experiments regarding basic income around the globe. Most of the experiments offer basic income as a solution to automation, lack of disposable income, benefit traps, or a bloated bureaucracy (cf. Oxford University 2016; King 2016; Amadeo 2018; The Next Era 2017).

But the idea of a basic income is actually not new. There were famous advocates in the last century. For example, Martin Luther King, Jr. (1967) said a guaranteed income would abolish poverty, which means reducing inequality as well. Economist Milton Friedman proposed a so-called "negative income tax", which supports the poor by giving them a tax credit if their income fell below a minimum level (cf. Amadeo 2018; Birnbaum 2016). Over history, this exceedingly simple idea of a basic income has a surprisingly diverse pedigree. In the past it has been independently thought up under a variety of names such as "territorial dividend" or "state bonus," for example; also "demogrant," "citizen's wage," "universal benefit" or "basic income." These concepts could primarily help the people who will not be able to find work and protect them from falling under the poverty line in a future with AI-driven automation. Advocates argue that it leads to greater economic security among vulnerable citizens. By that, it could be useful to keep negative side-effects such as depredations away from everyday life. In this way, it would prepare for a world with increasing divisions and social conflicts between elites and unemployed masses as described in chapter eight (cf. Maney 2017; Van Parijs Basic Income 2004; Dahlbom 2017; Makridakis 2017:19ff.; King 2016; Ito 2018).

The general idea of a basic income has many different faces, so the devil will be in the details, as it is said because concepts already differ on who receives the income (cf. De Wispelaere et al 2004: 1f.). Focussing on details of a basic income and what type of guaranteed income suits each country best are beyond the scope of this chapter.
The following part of the chapter will look at the most discussed type of a basic income and its general advantages and disadvantages for society. Based on most parts of the definitions in the literature, it supports all citizens with modest, yet unconditional, income paid by a political community.

> "Basic income is a periodic cash payment unconditionally delivered to all on an individual basis, without means test or work requirement." (Birnbaum 2016).

Notably, this definition of the Basic Income Earth Network is the most common in the literature. It includes five common characteristics based. Firstly, it is periodic, and it is paid at regular intervals, not as a one-off grant. Secondly, it is a cash payment, which allows those who receive it to decide what they spend it on (so it is not, therefore, paid rather in vouchers dedicated to a specific use). Thirdly, it is paid on an individual basis, not, for instance, to households. Fourthly, it is universal and paid to all, without a specific test or requirements. Fifthly, it has an unconditional character, so it has to be paid without a requirement to work or to demonstrate willingness-to-work (cf. Bien 2018; Birnbaum 2016).

The next part of the chapter will discuss the advantages and disadvantages of a basic income. Advocates suggest a basic income could stand to alleviate poverty on a global scale, especially regarding tech and automation. Wages have remained largely stagnant for a long time so that despite technological leaps forward, many employees have not felt as many tangible benefits as might be expected. But services or even products do not just need to be assembled. They need to be bought. For this, a guaranteed income could be a solution for solving upcoming challenges. It would enable workers to wait for a better or more suitable job or negotiate better wages. With a basic income, individuals could also improve their marketability by going back to school and taking some time off in case of illness. Apart from the high cost of such social support, the simplicity of the program means it would also cost governments less, also by cutting down on bureaucracy.

In terms of disadvantages, if everyone in the society suddenly received a basic income, it could lead to inflation and many people would immediately spend the money, which drives up demand. In consequence, retailers would have to order more goods, and manufacturers would try to produce more. But if manufacturers were not able to increase the supply, they would raise prices. In consequence higher prices would make the basics unaffordable for lower-income people, so in the long run, a guaranteed income would not meet its main goal to increase living standards, abolish poverty, or reduce social inequality. Furthermore, there might be different challenges for how to finance it, because the whole payments would be extremely expensive for the governments. Another aspect may be the risk that it could remove the incentive to work hard. Recipients might prefer a life with a free income rather than applying for an available job. The last aspect is that especially poor countries could get left behind because they could not afford a basic income for their societies. Therefore it could be seen as a utopian ideal of developed countries only.

Regions that are already struggling to provide for example basic services and infrastructure, implementing this is simply an impossibility, and just another way for poor countries to get left behind (cf. Amadeo 2018; King 2018).

As already mentioned, different localities have been considering or experimenting with the concept of a basic income rather than an income itself. While there are many reasons for welcoming basic income experiments, it has to be recognized as well that these structural connections and the dynamic long-term effects of basic income in the wider population can still not be fully captured (cf. Birnbaum 2016; Ito 2018). All in all, the outlined basic income can be seen as a possible solution to a long-term scenario described in chapter seven, even if there is no consensus about its need and effect on future society. Regarding the exact realization of such a basic income and its financing basis, difficult challenges can still be identified and have to be examined more detailed within another research.

9. Critical Review

This chapter shall briefly discuss some critical aspects of the arguments presented in this thesis, limited to AI, the theoretical approach deployed, the resulting analysis and therefore on the thesis and its results.
The first starting point here is the distinction between weak and strong AI. On the one hand, a better description, and categorization of AI is required, considering the weak definitions used today. However, the categorization undertaken here is also vague and artificial. For one reason it is vague due to the lack of real-world experience with AI. A large number of use cases certainly already exists, but they will rise fast and will, therefore, allow better analysis and a more precise categorization of AI forms and characteristics in the future. But is also artificial for the lack of a very clear definition of boundaries, i.e. where precisely do weak AI end and strong AI start. Moreover, in practice, the borders are likely to more fluent, the strength and scope of AI depending on the technology, depth and finally the intelligence of an application.

In this conjunction, it shall be noted that today it is still disputed if strong AI actually does already exist. Such a consensus exists on weak AI, but the focus of this work was placed on the effects of strong AI. A discussion of a technological phenomenon which does not exist according to contributors to the debate might be considered as a weakness. However, such line of argument might be subject to AI definition: Some would call forms of AI as weak which are, however, labeled as strong AI in this thesis. Moreover, an argument that – subject to the AI definition used – strong AI does not yet actually exist in the information economy does not preclude that it will be deployed. This needs to be verified in the years to come.

Considering the concept of the information society used in this thesis, the criticism that the concept is too broad, encompassing while unprecise and often rather used as an "umbrella" term is valid. The question is if the concept of the information society is actually a concept, given even the seemingly absence of a consensus of on definitions and terminology as argued in chapter three.

Further, the concept has been developed in the second half of the 20th century. Although the concept seeks – by and large – to carry forward developments in society incorporating information technology, by no means it is assured that the concept would hold in the 21st century, in particular considering the ever faster speed of technological advancement and the potential application of strong AI. Further research must show if the concept of the information society can be further adapted to current and future developments or if an entirely new approach is required to enhance our understanding and to positively contribute to the academic and non-academic debate.

Further criticism may be applied to other concepts used in this paper, such as the information economy, information sector or the knowledge worker. Considering, for example, the information sector it may be argued that not just a qualitative but also quantitative analysis should be conducted, researching the real economy using e.g. statistical means. Then a better assessment on the validity and viability of concept could be made. This also holds for the concepts information worker and knowledge worker.

Looking at the analysis conducted here, a much broader but also deeper analysis is warranted to better be able to confirm or weaken the validity of hypotheses brought forward. For instance, would industry sectors could be analyzed in far more detail, thus improving the method while yielding more insights.

The discussion on the effects of AI also needs to better incorporate other countervailing arguments as could be done within the scope of this research. For instance, some contributors argue that strong AI will never destroy all jobs because AI-guided by human intelligence will always be more productive than AI working on its own. In addition, AI will more so augment human workers in many ways rather than replace them (cf. Fraser 2017; Braga et al. 2017: 2f.). Others argue AI might receive a larger place in the sun than warranted, using terms such as "AI winter" to highlight their case (cf. Pieniewski 2018), however, putting an argument forth that there might be possible crash expectations of AI in the future.

Finally, it shall be noted that a deeper and more encompassing analysis of the supposed consequences of strong AI is required. This is needed for several reasons, e.g. to incorporate country-specific elements, be it their political systems, state of economic development, readiness to adjust to changes, to mention a few factors. Such an extended analysis would also be a necessary precondition for developing more appropriate and less generic policy strategies.

10. Conclusion

The first goal of this thesis was – using the hypotheses developed – to analyze the potential impact of strong AI within and on the information economy. The findings resulting from this analysis have been summarised in the interim conclusions and subsequently verified against current studies and additional literature, showing a principal validity and reliability of the developed hypotheses.

The main findings shall be briefly recapitulated here as follows: Strong AI has the potential to disrupt the main subdivisions of the information economy and the occupational structures resulting from today's information societies will be affected by massive labor market changes due to strong AI. Also, the use of AI will result in profound changes in the required skills sets for knowledge workers as well as changing the ways and means to do their jobs. Strong AI is yielding more results and higher productivity as a knowledge worker could achieve, but the scope and extent is strongly subject to the degree of complexity of individual jobs in and across industry segments. In the first wave of AI deployment, the productivity of knowledge workers will be increased using intelligent systems and applications in the form of human-machine integration. In a second wave, strong AI could even substitute knowledge workers by providing better efficiency and productivity as a knowledge worker could achieve.

Using those interim results, two possible scenarios interpolating the present into the future. The first focussed on a short to the mid-term time frame which described an increased human-machine integration and transformation. Then we discussed a mid to long-term scenario producing more drastic effects with regard to unemployment, inequality, and aspects of social security. This discussion showed that thesis one put forward in chapter comprehensively applies to the mid and long-term scenario, namely: Strong AI can mean the erosion of today's information economy by affecting employment in the way that it will destroy more jobs than creating new ones for the same educated workforce.
It is not a new phenomenon that technical changes produce shifts in job structures. Old jobs and even complete occupations vanish, but others are created without in the long-term reducing the total employment level. But this time, this could be different. Strong AI will substitute many jobs while fare lesser jobs than being substitute will be created. Rising unemployment would be the result. This trend might be aggravated by skill requirements in an ICT economy under strong AI. Requirements might become so high that fewer and fewer members of the workforce can fulfill them. Thus, even if new, different areas for work and thus jobs could be created, they cannot be filled due to their vast skill requirements not even very highly skilled knowledge workers can provide.
Further, if AI leads to job losses on a massive scale and to decreasing overall employment levels, the entire fabric or work and labor as a value system might change or erode. Work as the paramount means for individual subsistence might cease to exist for large portions of the labor force. Unemployment, income losses but also the loss of individual status, means to pursue non-work activities, the "sense of working", fulfillment, social environment and interaction, the lack of feeling "being useful" might erode believe in the entire economic and finally into the political system.
Based on the analysis of this piece of work, several societal changes and challenges produced and caused by strong AI came to the fore. These have been used to develop options for political strategies also arguing that timely, goal-oriented actions seem to be required as of now. Against the theoretical framework, the use cases and – albeit – first and initial empirical sources presented, only then a more positive development on the information society deeply impacted by strong AI may materialize.

In this conjunction, also the second hypothesis of chapter 6.2. can be verified. To encounter the highly likely effects of AI and in particular strong AI, governments should seek actions to shape the effects of tech-

nological changes on the society and facilitate more equal distribution of the positive effects of technical changes.
The following quote summarizes all the mentioned developments and the beginning of strong AI and helps to answer this thesis:

> "AI is both the bad witch and good witch—destroyer and creator." (Maney 2017).

States, in the meaning of political actors incorporating many aspects of social interaction, have to develop models or strategies for actions. On the one hand, to benefit from the options presented by technological changes. But also, on the other hand, to mitigate the negative effects such as potential mass unemployment in the mid to long-term. There might be many complex and intertwined solutions, which could not be discussed in this research in any real depth. But the paper created themes for solutions to the challenges created on the developments in the field of strong AI.

Therefore, in the light of increasing human-machine integration taking place in the next years, policies should be formulated and implemented in the short to mid-term. Governments should emphasize measures such as retraining, preparing the workforce and thus large-scale investment in education.
Currently, the world's most developed economies suffer limited employment issues, not to speak of mass unemployment. Thus, to better pre-empt such scenarios while at the same time create the foundations to benefit from AI, actions should be taken now. These, however, must be designed to meet the specifics of each national economy.

> "We have no choice but to make policy of what see in the world right now." (Rotman 2018).

The introduction of a basic income „just" because AI is around the corner might be a too early step to take today. The primary target should be to enable lower-skilled workers and knowledge workers alike to be prepared for occupation challenges inside their current jobs as well as for new job scenarios to be found an created through automation:

> As Voltaire said: "Work saves a man from the three great evils: boredom, vice, and need." (Deutsch 2017).

The focus should be to preserve human labor, a decisive factor here being education, reinforced by training. This creates the fundamentals to learn new skills, master tasks and thus new jobs including the requirements placed by them on employees. Looking at the analysis in chapter five, the chances presented in the education sector could be just one example. Digital content and methods for teachers and students alike, an environment which does not just enable to strongly supports life-long learning seem to be highly appropriate. All in all, the combination between education and retraining programs are important strategies for the future of today's information societies, in which the human-machine symbiosis will be essential. For this, it is important to determine how people can work together in an optimal relationship with robots and AI-driven applications. This suggests that both humans and machines should better understand the opposing part. All in all, the synthesis of tasks getting done by machines and others by people will be even smarter than just one side of the equation.

Only if such guiding, supportive measures fail to counter effects such as mass unemployment and even bigger unequal income distribution aggravated by strong-AI driven automation, other country-specific provisions should be taken into consideration.

References

Monographs, Contributions to Anthologies and Journals

Alpcan, Tansu/ Erfani, Sarah/ Leckie, Christopher (2017): Toward the Starting Line: A Systems Engineering Approach to Strong AI, University of Melbourne: Victoria.

Arriaga, Patricia (1985): Toward a critique of the information economy, in: Media, Culture & Society, vol. 7(3).

Baker, Jamie (2018): 2018 A Legal Research Odyssey: Artificial Intelligence as disruptor, Texas Tech University School of Law, Law Lib. J. 110(1).

Bell, Daniel (1973, 1976): The Coming of Post-Industrial Society: A Venture in Social Forecasting, Basic Books: New York.

Bell, Daniel (1980): The Social Framework of the Information Society, in: The Complete Guide to the New Technology and Its Impact on Society, MIT Press: Cambridge.

Beniger, James (1986): The Control Revolution: Technological and Economic Origins of the Information Society, Harvard University Press: Cambridge.

Berthoud, Gérald/ Kündig, Albert/ Sitter-Liver, Beat (2003): Informationsgesellschaft, Geschichten und Wirklichkeit, Academic Press: Fribourg.

Birnbaum, Simon (2016): Basic income, Oxford University Press: Oxford.

Bode Ulrich (1997): Die Informationsgesellschaft, in: Die Informationsrevolution, Gabler Verlag: Wiesbaden.

Braga, Adriana/ Logan, Robert (2017): The Emperor of Strong AI Has No Clothes: Limits to Artificial Intelligence, in: Journal Information, 8 (156).

Brinkley Ian/ Fauth Rebecca/ Mahdon Michelle/ Theodoropouloum Sotiria (2009): Knowledge Workers and Knowledge Work, The Work Foundation: London.

Brougham, David/ Haar, Jarrod (2017): Smart Technology, Artificial Intelligence, Robotics, and Algorithms (STARA): Employees' perceptions of our future workplace, in: Journal of Management & Organization, 24:2.

Brynjolfsson, Erik/ McAfee, Andrew (2014): The-Second Machine Age, Norton and Company: New York.

Brynjolfsson, Erik/ Rock, Daniel/ Syverson, Chad (2017): Artificial Intelligence and the Modern Productivity Paradox: A Clash of Expectations and Statistics, NBER Working Paper No. 24001.

Buchanan, Ben/ Miller, Taylor (2017): Machine Learning for Policymakers, What It Is and Why It Matters, Belfer Center for Science and International Affairs: Cambridge, Massachusetts.

Castells, Manuel (1996): Information Age: Economy, Society and Culture, Volume I: The Rise of the Network Society, Blackwell: Oxford.

Colman, Andrew (2015): Weak AI n. A. Dictionary of Psychology, Oxford University Press.

Colman, Andrew (2015b): Strong AI n. A Dictionary of Psychology, Oxford University Press.

Dahlbom, Bo (2017): The Future of Work, in: Proceedings 2017, 1(3).

Davenport, Thomas H. (2005): Thinking For A Living: How to Get Better Performance and Results From Knowledge Workers, Harvard Business School Press: Boston.

David, Paul/ Foray, Dominique (2003): Economic Fundamentals of the Knowledge Society, in: Policy Futures in Education, Vol. 1(1).

De Wispelaere, Jurgen/ Stirton, Lindsay (2004): The Many Faces of Universal Basic Income, in: The Pollitical Quarterly 75(3).

Dirican, Cüneyt (2015): The Impacts of Robotics, Artificial Intelligence On Business and Economics, in: Procedia - Social and Behavioral Sciences 195.

Dolata, Ulrich/ Schrape, Jan-Felix (2012): Internet, Mobile Devices und die Transformation der Medien. Radikaler Wandel als schrittweise Rekonfiguration. Berlin: Edition Sigma 2012.

Dostal, Werner (1995): Die Informatisierung der Arbeitswelt – Multimedia, offene Arbeitsformen und Telearbeit, in: Mitteilungen aus der Arbeitsmarkt- und Berufsforschung, 4/1995.

Drucker, Peter (1954): Landmarks of Tomorrow. A Report on the New 'Post-Modern'World, Transaction Publisher: London.

Drucker, Peter (1959): The Landmarks of Tomorrow, Harper and Row: New York.

Drucker, Peter (1999): Management im 21. Jahrhundert, Econ: München.

Drucker, Peter F. (1969): The Age of Discontinuity, Guidelines to our Changing Society, Heinemann: London.

Drucker, Peter F. (2011): Post-capitalist Society, Routledge: New York.

Duff, Alistair (1996): A note on the origins of the „information society“, in: Journal of Information Science, 22 (2).

Duff, Alistair (1998): Daniel Bells Theory of the Inormation Society, in: Journal of Information Science, 24(6).

Dugherty, Paul/ Wilson, James (2018): Human+Machine: Reimagining Work in the Age of AI, Harvard Business Review Press: Cambrdge, MA.

Eichhorst, Werner/ Buhlmann, Florian (2015): Die Zukunft der Arbeit und der Wandel der Arbeitswelt, Institute for the Study of Labor, IZA Standpunkte No. 77, IZA: Bonn.

Engelhardt, Anina/ Kajetzke, Laura (2010): Handbuch Wissensgesellschaft: Theorien, Themen und Probleme, Transcript Verlag: Bielefeld.

Ertel, Wolfgang (2016): Grundkurs künstliche Intelligenz. Springer: Wiesbaden.

Esteva, Andre/ Kuprel, Brett/ Novoa, Roberto/ Ko, Justin/ Swetter, Susan/ Blau, Helen/ Thrun, Sebastian (2017): Dermatologist-Level Classification of Dermatologist-Level Classification of Skin Cancer with Deep Neural Networks, in: Nature, Vol. 542, No. 7639.

Frey, Carl Benedikt/ Osborne, Michel (2013): The Future of Employment, Oxford Martin Programme on Technology and Employment, Oxford University: Oxford.

Fuchs, Christian (2012): Capitalism or information society? The fundamental question of the present structure of society, in: European Journal of Social Theory 16(4).

Furman, Jason (2016): Is This Time Different? The Opportunities and Challenges of Artificial Intelligence, New York University: New York.

Gentsch, Peter (2018): Künstliche Intelligenz für Sales, Marketing und Service. Springer: Wiesbaden.

Gershenfeld et al. (2017): Designing Reality: How to Survive and Thrive in the Third Digital Revolution, Basic Books: New York.

Glowalla Ulrich (1996): Menschliche Kommunikation in der Informationsgesellschaft. In: Deutscher Multimedia Kongreß '96, Springer: Berlin, Heidelberg.

Heinen, Nicolaus/ Heuer, Alexander/ Schautschick, Philipp (2017): Künstliche Intelligenz und der Faktor Arbeit, in: Wirtschaftsdienst 2017 ZBW, 97.(10).

Hummert, Henning/ Traum, Anne/ Müller, Christoph/ Nerdinger, Friedemann (2018): Digitalisierung – Auswirkungen auf das Individuum, White Paper Series No.2., Universität Rostock: Rostock.

Jarrahi, Mohammad Hossein (2018): Artificial Intelligence and the Future of Work: Human-AI Symbiosis in Organizational Decision Making, Kelley School of Business, Indiana University.

Kamps, Klaus (1999): Elektronische Demokratie? Perspektiven politischer Partizipation, Westdeutscher Verlag: Wiesbaden.

Karvalics, Laszlo Z. (2007): Information Society – what is it exactly? The meaning, history and conceptual framework of an expression, Budapest.

Kasperkiewicz, Witold (2004): The concept of an information society in the european union, in: Acta Universitatis Lodziensis, Folia Oeconomica 182.

Kidd, Alison (1994): The Marks are on the Knowledge Worker, in: Human Factors in Computing Systems, Boston, Vol.4.

Kleinsteuber, Hans J. (1999): Die Informationsgesellschaft - Eine Gesellschaft ohne Information über sich selbst?, in: P. Donges et al. (eds.), Globalisierung der Medien?, Westdeutscher Verlag: Wiesbaden.

Klotz, Michael (2003): Informationsgesellschaft, in: Lexikon Electronic Business, R. Oldenburg: München-Wien.

Klotz, Michael (2009): Von der Informationsgesellschaft zum Informationsarbeiter, in: SIMAT Arbeitspapiere, No. 01-09-002.

Kurzweil, Ray (2005). The Singularity is Near: When Humans Transcend Biology, Viking Press: New York City.

Lowe, G.S. (2002): Leveraging the skills of Knowledge Workers, Isuma: Spring.

Machlup, Fritz (1962): The production and distribution of knowledge in the United States, Princeton University Press: New York.

Machlup, Fritz (1962): The production and distribution of knowledge in the United States, Princeton: Princeton, NJ, University Press 1962.

Macmillen (2017): The future of work, in: Nature Vol.550(7676).

Makridakis, Spyros (2017): The Forthcoming Artificial Intelligence (AI) Revolution: Its Impact on Society and Firms, Neapolis University Hephaestus Repository: Paphos.

Maney, Kevin (2016): How Artificial Intelligence and Robots Will Radically Transform the Economy, in: Newsweek, Vol.167, 21.

Martin, Bill (2005): Information society revisited: from vision to reality, in: Journal of Information Science, 31 (1).

Marwala, Tshilidzi/ Hurwitz, Evan (2017): Artificial Intelligence and Economic Theory: Skynet in the Market, Springer International Publishing.

Mason, Paul (2015): Post-Capitalism: A Guide to Our Future, Allen Lane Penguin Books: London.

Masuda, Yoneji (1980): Emerging Information Society in Japan. In The Information Society as Post-Industrial Society, Institute for the Information Society: Tokyo.

Masuda, Yoneji (1981): The Information Society as Post-industrial Society, World Future Society: Bethesda.

May, Christopher (2000): Knowledge workers, teleworkers and plumbers: Labour in the global information economy, in: Online-proceedings of the 41st annual convention of the International Studies Association.

McKinsey (2017): Artificial Intelligence the next digital frontier?, McKinsey Global Institute.

Mladkova, Ludmila/ Zouharova, Jarmila/ Novy, Jindrich (2015): Motivation and Knowledge Workers, in: Procedia Social and Behavioral Sciences 207.

Murphy, Kevin (2012): Machine Learning, A Probhabilistic Perspective. The MIT Press: Cambridge, Massachusetts.

O'Neil, Cathy (2016): Weapons of Math Destruction: How Big Data Increases Inequality and Threatens Democracy, Allen Lane: London.

Pearson (2016): Intelligence unleashed: An argument for AI in education, UCL Knowledge Lab: London.

Piovesan/ Ntiri (2018): Adjudication by algorithm: The risks and benefits of artificial intelligence in judicial decision-making, in: The advocates' journal, Spring 2018.

Porat, Marc Uri (1977): The information economy: definition and measurement. U.S. Department of Commerce, Office of Telecommunication, in: OT Special Publication 77-12 (1).

Porat, Marc Uri (1998): The Information Economy: Definition and Measurement, in: Rise of the Knowledge Worker, Butterworth-Heinemann: Boston.

Reboul, C. et al. (2006): Managing Knowledge Workers: The KWP Matrix, Conference Proceedings MOMAN 06: Prague.

Reich, Robert (1992): The Work of Nations, Vintage Books: New York.

Reinecke, Christiane (2010): Wissensgesellschaft und Informationsgesellschaft, in: Docupedia-Zeitgeschichte, 11., 2/10.

Reinhardt, Wolfgang; Schmidt, Benedikt; Sloep, Peter; Drachsler, Hendrik (2011): Knowledge Worker Roles and Actions – Results of Two Empirical Studies, in: Knowledge and Process Management, 18 (3).

Rieber, Daniel (2017): Mobile Marketing, Grundlagen, Strategien, Instrumente. Springer: Berlin.

Roßnagel, Alexander/ Wedde, Peter/ Hammer, Volker/ Pordesch, Ulrich (1990, 2009): Die Verletzlichkeit der Informationsgesellschaft, Westdeutscher Verlag: Opladen.

Rouhiainen, Lasse (2018): Artificial Intelligence: 101 Things You Must Know Today About Our Future, CreateSpace Independent Publishing Platform.

Sarkar, Atrisha (2018): A Brandom-ian view of Reinforcement Learning towards strong-AI, University of Waterloo: Ontario.

Sesink, Werner (2012): Menschliche und künstliche Intelligenz, Der kleine Unterschied, Stuttgart.

Steinbicker, Jochen (2011): Zur Theorie der Informationsgesellschaft, Verschiedene Ansätze – was gemeinsam/ insgesamt?, Springer: Wiesbaden.

Svarc, Jadranka (2016): The knowledge worker is dead: What about professions?, in: Current Sociology, Vol. 64(3).

Sveiby, Karl (1997): The new organizational wealth: Managing and measuring knowledge- based assets, Berrett-Koehler: San Francisco.

Toffler, Alwin (1990): Powershift: Knowledge, Wealth and Violence at the Edge of the 21st Century, Bantam Books: New York.

Trauth, Eileen M. (2000): The culture of an information economy, Kluwer Academic Publishers: Boston.

Tully, Claus J. (1994): Lernen in der Informationsgesellschaft: Informelle Bildung durch Computer , Westdeutscher Verlag: Opladen.

U.S. Government (2016): Artificial Intelligence, Automation, and the Economy, Executive Office of the President: Washington D.C.

Van Parijs, Philippe (2004): Basic Income: A simple and powerful idea for the twenty-first century, in: Sage Journals, Politics and Society Vol.32(1).

Wahlmüller-Schiller, Christine (2017): Künstliche Intelligenz – wohin geht die Reise?, in: Elektrotechnik & Informationstechnik, 134/7.

Webster, Frank (2006, 2014): Theories of the Information Society, Routledge: New York.

Wedde, Peter/ Hammer, Volker/ Poresch, Ulrich (1990): Die Verletzlichkeit der 'Informationsgesellschaft', Westdeutscher Verlag: Opladen.

Magazines and Online Sources

Accenture (2016): Country Spotlights, Why AI is the Future of Growth, online: https://www.accenture.com/us-en/insight-artificial-intelligence-future-growth (last access: 07-31-2018).

AI100 (2017): Artificial Intelligence Index - 2017 Annual Report, Stanford University, online: https://aiindex.org/2017-report.pdf (last access: 07-31-2018).

Amadeo, Kimberly (2018): Universal Basic Income, Its Pros and Cons With Examples, online: https://www.thebalance.com/universal-basic-income-4160668 (last access: 07-31-2018).

Avery, Adam (2018): Artificial Intelligence Promises a Personalized Education for All, online unter: http://www.theatlantic.com/sponsored/vmware-2017/personalized-education/1667/ (last access: 07-31-2018).

Bajpai, Prableen (2017): How Facebook Is Using Artificial Intelligence, online: http://www.nasdaq.com/article/how-facebook-is-using-artificial-intelligence-cm848218 (last access: 07-31-2018).

Baron, Ethan (2016): Silicon Valley Waves of Innovation, online: http://www.siliconvalley.com/2016/12/18/silicon-valleys-savior-and-next-revolution-artificial- intelligence/ (last access: 07-31-2018).

Bashforth, George (2018): Is artificial intelligence the future of financial services? , online: http://www.caymanfinancialreview.com/2018/01/29/is-artificial-intelligence-the-future-of-financial-services/ (last access: 07-31-2018).

Berkman Klein Center (2017): Global AI Dialogue Series, online: http://cyber.harvard.edu/node/100129 (last access: 07-31-2018).

Bhardwaj, Gunjan (2018): How AI Can Revolutionize Financial Services, online: https://www.etftrends.com/robotics-ai-channel/how-ai-can-revolutionize-financial-services/ (last access: 07-31-2018).

Bien (2018): About basic income, online: https://basicincome.org/basic-income/ (last access: 07-31-2018).

Braun, Alexander (2015): Digitale Trend: Industrien der Transformation, online: https://www.creativeconstruction.de/blog/digitale-trends-industrien-der-digitalen-transformation-banking-fintech-quantified-self-cars-energy-health/ (last access: 07-31-2018).

Business Dictionary (2018): Information Services, online: http://www.busine ssdictionary.com/definition/information-services.html (last access: 07-31-2018).

Cambridge Dictionary (2018): Information economy, online: https://dictionary .cambridge.org/de/worterbuch/englisch/information-economy (last access: 07-31-2018).

Carter, Shan/ Nielsen, Michael (2018): Using Artificial Intelligence to Augment Human Intelligence, online: https://distill.pub/2017/aia/ (last access: 07-31-2018).

Chowdhry, Amit (2018): How Artificial Intelligence Is Going To Affect The Financial Industry In 2018, online: https://www.forbes.com/sites/amitchow dhry/2018/02/26/clinc-artificial-intelligence/#6a5ff48f481f (last access: 07-31-2018).

Clifford, Catherine (2016): Elon Musk: Robots will take your jobs, government will have to pay your wage, online: https://www.cnbc.com/201 6/11/04/elon-musk-robots-will-take-your-jobs-government-will-have-to-pay-your-wage.html (last access: 07-31-2018).

Columbus, Louis (2017): 80% Of Enterprises Are Investing In AI Today, online: https://www.forbes.com/sites/louiscolumbus/2017/10/16/80-of-enterprises-are-investing-in-ai-today/#30444d7e4d8e (last access: 07-31-2018).

Condliffe, Jamie (2018): The company that made smartphones smart now wants to give them built-in AI, online: https://www.technologyreview.com/ s/610182/the-company-that-made-smartphones-smart-now-wants-to-give-them-built-in-ai/ (last access: 07-31-2018).

Confino, Jo (2014): Radical new economic system will emerge from collapse of capitalism, online: https://www.theguardian.com/sustainable-business/ 2014/nov/07/radical-new-economic-system-will-emerge-from-collapse-of-capitalism (last access: 07-31-2018).

Coughlin, Tom (2017): How AI will make smartphones much smarter, online: https://venturebeat.com/2017/06/29/how-ai-will-make-smartphones-much-smarter/ (last access: 07-31-2018).

D´Monte, Leslie (2018): AI is a very surprising tech, which makes its future hard to predict: Bruce Schneier, online: https://www.livemint.com/AI/Vb4 RIepCjrd8rwfZyVz7pN/AI-is-a-very-surprising-tech-which-makes-its-future-hard-t.html (last access: 07-31-2018).

Data Collective (2017): Standing on the Shore: How AI is Disrupting the World's largest Industries, online: https://medium.com/data-collective/ standing-on-the-shore-how-ai-is-disrupting-the-worlds-largest-industries-38df7430a543 (last access: 07-31-2018).

Data Collective (2017): Standing on the Shore*: How AI is Disrupting the World's largest Industries, online: https://medium.com/@dcvc/standing-on-the-shore-how-ai-is-disrupting-the-worlds-largest-industries-38df7430a543 (last access: 07-31-2018).

Deloitte Digital and Heads! (2015): Überlebensstrategie „Digital Leadership", online: https://www2.deloitte.com/content/dam/Deloitte/at/Documents/ strategy/ueberlebensstrategie-digital-leadership_final.pdf (last access: 07-31-2018).

Dempsey, Katharine (2017): Economic and Social Impact of AI Takes Center Stage: The AI Boom Is Upon Us, But At What Social Cost?, online: https://washingtonspectator.org/dempsey-ai/ (last access: 07-31-2018).

Depp, Michael (2018): Will AI End Up Poaching Broadcast Jobs?, online: https://tvnewscheck.com/article/113112/will-ai-end-up-poaching-broadcast-jobs/ (last access: 07-31-2018).

De Waele, Rudy (2016): How AI is disrupting the world's largest industries, online: http://www.techvshuman.com/2016/08/22/how-ai-is-disrupting-the-worlds-largest- industries/ (last access: 07-31-2018).

Donovan, David (2017): The Rise of AI First World in Financial Services, online: https://www.finextra.com/blogposting/14386/the-rise-of-ai-first-world-in-financial-services (last access: 07-31-2018).

Dörner, Stephan (2017): Digitalisierung: Wer jetzt nicht exponentiell denkt, droht unterzugehen, online: https://t3n.de/news/digitalisierung-exponentiell -singularity-820706/ (last access: 07-31-2018).

EmTech (2018): AI and robotics are changing the future of work. Are you ready?, online: https://events.technologyreview.com/emtech/next/18/# section-schedule (last access: 07-31-2018).

Faggella, Daniel (2017): Examples of Artificial Intelligence in Education, online: https://www.techemergence.com/examples-of-artificial-intelligence-in-education/ (last access: 07-31-2018).

Financial Stability Board (2017): Artificial intelligence and machine learning in financial services, online: http://www.fsb.org/2017/11/artificial-intelligence-and-machine-learning-in-financial-service/ (last access: 07-31-2018).

Forbes (2017): McKinsey's State Of Machine Learning And AI, 2017, online: https://www.google.de/amp/s/www.forbes.com/sites/louiscolumbus/2017/07/09/mckinseys-state-of-machine-learning-and-ai-2017/amp/ (last access: 07-31-2018).

Fortunato et al. (2017): Noisy networks for exploration, online unter: https://arxiv.org/abs/1706.10295 (last access: 07-31-2018).

Fraser, Jeff (2017): A Primer on AI in Financial Services, online: https://medium.com/@jeffrey.fraser/primer-on-ai-in-financial-services-686640bd0a61 (last access: 07-31-2018).

Freedman, David (2016): Basic Income: A Sellout of the American Dream, online: https://www.technologyreview.com/s/601499/basic-income-a-sellout-of-the-american-dream/ (last access: 07-31-2018).

Fritschle, Matthew (2017): How AI Is Changing Digital Advertising, online: https://www.aumcore.com/blog/2017/11/22/how-ai-is-changing-digital-advertising/ (last access: 07-31-2018).

Fronda, Francisco (2017): The Dawn of AI in Broadcast and Media, online: https://www.media-power.it/site/it/newsarticle.php?title=The-Dawn-of-AI-in-Broadcast-and-Media (last access: 07-31-2018).

Fuertes, Rechelle (2017): Smartphone AI: The Trend That Will Make Future Phones Smarter, online: https://edgylabs.com/smartphone-ai-the-trend-that-will-make-future-phones-smarter (last access: 07-31-2018).

Greenwald, Ted (2011): How Smart Machines Like iPhone 4S Are Quietly Changing Your Industry: https://www.forbes.com/sites/tedgreenwald/2011/10/13/how-smart-machines-like-iphone-4s-are-quietly-changing-your-industry/#34c153a4598f (last access: 07-31-2018).

Helbing, Dirk et al. (2017): Will Democracy Survive Big Data and Artificial Intelligence?, online: https://www.scientificamerican.com/article/will-democracy-survive-big-data-and-artificial-intelligence/ (last access: 07-31-2018).

Herget, Steffen (2018): Machine learning and AI: How smartphones get even smarter, online: https://www.androidpit.com/machine-learning-and-ai-on-smartphones (last access: 07-31-2018).

Hindu Business Line (2017): Artificial Intelligence is the engine of the fourth industrial revolution, online: http://www.thehindubusinessline.com/info-tech/artificial-intelligence-is-the-engine-of-the-fourth-industrial-revolution/article9820230.ece (last access: 07-31-2018).

Houser, Kristin (2017): Tomorrow's Teachers, online: https://futurism.com/ai-teachers-education-crisis/ (last access: 07-31-2018).

https://www.idc.com/getdoc.jsp?containerId=prUS41878616 (last access: 07-31-2018).

IDC (2016): Worldwide Cognitive Systems and Artificial Intelligence Revenues Forecast to Surge Past $47 Billion in 2020, According to New IDC Spending Guide

Ingham, Lucy (2018): Stephen Hawking: "The Rise of Powerful AI Will Be Either the Best or the Worst Thing Ever to Happen to Humanity", online: http://factor-tech.com/feature/stephen-hawking-the-rise-of-powerful-ai-will-be-either-the-best-or-the-worst-thing-ever-to-happen-to-humanity/ (last access: 07-31-2018).

International Telecommunication Union (2017): Measuring the Information Society Report 2017 online: https://reliefweb.int/report/world/measuring-information-society-report-2017 (last access: 07-31-2018).

Ito, Joe (2018): The paradox of universal basic income, online: https://www.wired.com/story/the-paradox-of-universal-basic-income/ (last access: 07-31-2018).

Javelosa, June/ Houser, Kristin (2017): Major Firm Announces It's Replacing Its Employees with A.I., online: https://futurism.com/major-firm-announces-its-replacing-its-employees-with-a-i/ (last access: 07-31-2018).

KeepCoding 2017: How important is your smartphone in your life?, online: https://medium.com/@KeepCoding_/how-important-is-your-smartphone-in-your-life-28ec82fff721 (last access: 07-31-2018).

Kelnar (2016): The fourth industrial revolution: a primer on Artificial Intelligence (AI) online: https://medium.com/mmc-writes/the-fourth-industrial-revolution-a-primer-on-artificial-intelligence-ai-ff5e7fffcae1 (last access: 07-31-2018).

Kerns, Jeff (2017) What's the Difference Between AI and Machine Learning?, online: http://www.machinedesign.com/industrial-automation/what-s-difference-between-ai-and-machine-learning (last access: 07-31-2018).

King, Carrie (2016): Universal Basic Income: The Pros and Cons, online: https://journal.jobspotting.com/en/job-search/universal-basic-income/ (last access: 07-31-2018).

Kletzer, Lori (2018): The question with AI isn´t whether we´ll lose our jobs – it´s how much we´ll get paid, online: https://hbr.org/2018/01/the-question-with-ai-isnt-whether-well-lose-our-jobs-its-how-much-well-get-paid (last access: 07-31-2018).

Krasadakis, George (2017): Artificial Intelligence: the impact on employment and the workforce, online: https://medium.com/@gkrasadakis/artificial-intelligence-3c6d80072416 (last access: 07-31-2018).

Lant, Karla (2017): An Ad Agency Now Has the World's First AI Creative Director, online: https://futurism.com/an-ad-agency-now-has-the-worlds-first-ai-creative-director/ (last access: 07-31-2018).

Lant, Karla (2017b): Confirmed: AI Can Predict Heart Attacks and Strokes More Accurately Than Doctors, online: https://futurism.com/confirmed-ai-can-predict-heart-attacks-and-strokes-more-accurately-than-doctors/ (last access: 07-31-2018).

Lee, Hyea Won (2016): What is Korea's Strategy to Manage the Implications of Artificial Intelligence?, online: http://blogs.worldbank.org/ic4d/what-korea-s-strategy-manage-implications-artificial-intelligence (last access: 07-31-2018).

Lomas, Natasha (2018): The light and dark of AI-powered smartphones, online: https://techcrunch.com/2018/01/06/the-light-and-dark-of-aipowered -smartphones/?guccounter=1 (last access: 07-31-2018).

Lynch, Matthew 2018: 7 Roles For Artificial Intelligence In Education, online: https://www.thetechedvocate.org/7-roles-for-artificial-intelligence-in-education/ (last access: 07-31-2018).

Mahdawi, Arwa (2017): What jobs will still be around in 20 years? Read this to prepare your future, online: http://jobinthearts.com/jobs-will-still-around-20-years-read-prepare-future/ (last access: 07-31-2018).

Mahroum, Sami (2018): AI raises lots of questions. These are the ones we should be asking, online: https://www.weforum.org/agenda/2018/02/this-is-the-ai-debate-that-we-need-to-have (last access: 07-31-2018).

Maugain, Olivier (2017): How artificial intelligence is transforming advertising, online: http://www.marketing-interactive.com/how-artificial-intelligence-is-transforming-advertising/ (last access: 07-31-2018).

Metz, Rachel (2018): We still don't know much about the jobs the AI economy will make—or take, online: https://www.technologyreview.com/s/611329/we-still-dont-much-about-the-jobs-the-ai-economy-will-makeor-take/ (last access: 07-31-2018).

Metz, Rachel (2018b): Want to robot-proof your job? Here are some tips from experts in the field, online: https://www.technologyreview.com/s/611298/want-to-robot-proof-your-job-here-are-some-tips-from-experts-in-the-field/ (last access: 07-31-2018).

Microsoft (2018): Partnership on AI' formed by Google, Facebook, Amazon, IBM and Microsoft, online: https://www.theguardian.com/technology/2016/sep/28/google-facebook-amazon-ibm-microsoft-partnership-on-ai-tech-firms (last access: 07-31-2018).

Motte, Yann (2017): Artificial Intelligence: What's hot beyond buzzwords…, https://whatsnext.nuance.com/customer-experience/artificial-intelligence-whats-hot-beyond-buzzwords/ (last access: 07-31-2018).

Narrativ Science (2017): The Rise of AI in Financial Services, online: https://msenterprise.global.ssl.fastly.net/wordpress/2017/07/Narrative-Science-The-Rise-of-AI-in-Financial-Services.pdf (last access: 07-31-2018).

Narula, Gautam (2018): Everyday Examples of Artificial Intelligence and Machine Learning, online: https://www.techemergence.com/everyday-examples-of-ai/ (last access: 07-31-2018).

Newswire Europe 2016: Global Report Predicts EdTech Spend to Reach $252bn by 2020, online: https://www.prnewswire.com/news-releases/global-report-predicts-edtech-spend-to-reach-252bn-by-2020-580765301.html (last access: 07-31-2018).

Northeastern News (2018): Higher Education Must Change To Prepare Americans For Artificial Intelligence Revolution, online: https://news.northeastern.edu/2018/01/31/higher-education-must-change-to-prepare-americans-for-artificial-intelligence-revolution/ (last access: 07-31-2018).

Oxford University (2016): The future of work, online: https://medium.com/oxford-university/the-future-of-work-cf8a33b47285 (last access: 07-31-2018).

Oxford University (2018): New study shows nearly half of US jobs at risk of computerisation, http://www.eng.ox.ac.uk/about/news/new-study-shows-nearly-half-of-us-jobs-at-risk-of-computerisation (last access: 07-31-2018).

Philips, Avery (2018): The Future of AI and Education, online: https://insidebigdata.com/2018/05/13/future-ai-education/ (last access: 07-31-2018).

Popenici, Stefan/ Kerr, Sharon (2017): Exploring the impact of artificial intelligence on teaching and learning in higher education, Research and Practice in Technology Enhanced Learning Vol. 12, No.22.

Puget, Jean Francois (2017): What Is Artificial Intelligence?, online: https://www.ibm.com/developerworks/community/blogs/jfp/entry/997?lang=en (last access: 07-31-2018).

Rahman, Oliur (2018): AI Smartphones Will Soon Be Standard, Thanks to Machine Learning Chip, online: https://futurism.com/ai-smartphones-machine-learning-chip/ (last access: 07-31-2018).

Regalado, Antonio (2018): Seeing the mind of a robot in augmented reality, online: https://www.technologyreview.com/s/611296/seeing-the-mind-of-a-robot-in-augmented-reality/ (last access: 07-31-2018).

Reichert, Corinne (2017): AI will transform smartphones into 'intelligent phones': Huawei, online: https://www.zdnet.com/article/ai-will-transform-smartphones-into-intelligent-phones-huawei/ (last access: 07-31-2018).

Reinecke, Christiane 2010: Wissensgesellschaft und Informationsgesellschaft, Version: 1.0, in: Docupedia Zeitgeschichte, 11. Februar 2010, online:

http://docupedia.de/images/8/85/Wissensgesellschaft.pdf (last access: 07-31-2018).

Rotman, David (2017): The Relentless Pace of Automation, online: https://www.technologyreview.com/s/603465/the-relentless-pace-of-automation/ (last access: 07-31-2018).

Rouse, Margaret (2018): ICT information and communications technology, or technologies, online unter: https://searchcio.techtarget.com/definition/ICT-information-and-communications-technology-or-technologies (last access: 07-31-2018).

Rutkin, Aviva Hope (2013): Report Suggests Nearly Half of U.S. Jobs Are Vulnerable to Computerization, online: https://www.technologyreview.com /s/519241/report-suggests-nearly-half-of-us-jobs-are-vulnerable-to-computerization/ (last access: 07-31-2018).

Sandhana, Lakshmi 2013: 47% of US jobs under threat from computerization according to Oxford study, online: https://newatlas.com/half-of-us-jobs-computerized/29142/ (last access: 07-31-2018).

Schenker, Jennifer (2017): How AI is Disrupting Business, online: https://innovator.news/how-ai-is-disrupting-business-837406fd3be9 (last access: 07-31-2018).

Schrage, Michael (2017): 4 Models of AI to make decisions, online: https://hbr.org/2017/01/4-models-for-using-ai-to-make-decisions (last access: 07-31-2018).

Sigmoidal (2018): Artificial Intelligence in Finance, online: https://sigmoidal. io/real-applications-of-ai-in-finance/ (last access: 07-31-2018).

Simonite, Tom (2018): The Wired Guide To Artificial Intelligence, online https://www.wired.com/story/guide-artificial-intelligence/ (last access: 07-31-2018).

Souter, David (2018): Inside the Information Society: The road to artificial intelligence, online: https://www.apc.org/en/blog/inside-information-society-road-artificial-intelligence (last access: 07-31-2018).

Spira, Jonathan (2008): Knowledge worker: Do you related?, online: http://www.kmworld.com/Articles/News/News-Analysis/Knowledge-worker-Do-you-relate-40808.aspx (last access: 07-31-2018).

TeachThought Staff 2017: 10 Roles For Artifcial Intelligence In Education, online: https://www.teachthought.com/the-future-of-learning/10-roles-for-artificial-intelligence-in-education/ (last access: 07-31-2018).

Technative (2017): 7 Ways AI is set to impact financial services in 2018, online: https://www.technative.io/7-ways-ai-is-transforming-financial-services/ (last access: 07-31-2018).

The Business Communication (2018): Media (channels) of communication types of media communication, online: https://thebusinesscommunication.

com/types-of-media-communication/ (last access: 07-31-2018).

The Guardian (2017): Partnership on AI' formed by Google, Facebook, Amazon, IBM and Microsoft, online: https://voicebot.ai/2016/09/30/guardian-partnership-ai-formed-google-facebook-amazon-ibm-microsoft/ (last access: 07-31-2018).

The Next Era (2017): Everything You Ever Wanted to Know About Universal Basic Income, online: https://futurism.com/everything-you-ever-wanted-to-know-about-universal-basic-income/ (last access: 07-31-2018).

Tomer, Simon (2017): The State-of-the-Art of AI, online: https://chatbotnewsdaily.com/the-state-of-the-art-of-ai-d50512deb70a (last access: 07-31-2018).

Turbot, Sebastian 2017: Artificial Intelligence In Education: Don't Ignore It, Harness It!, online: https://www.forbes.com/sites/sebastienturbot/2017/08/22/artificial-intelligence-virtual-reality-education/#729c1c7a6c16 (last access: 07-31-2018).

Turner, Camilla (2014): Technology is biggest threat to employment, warns Larry Summers, online: https://www.telegraph.co.uk/finance/economics/10859041/Technology-is-biggest-threat-to-employment-warns-Larry-Summers.html (last access: 07-31-2018).

van der Touw, Willem/ Glitz, Oliver (2016): Starke und schwache künstliche Intelligenz, https://www.notch-interactive.com/de/blog/2016/11/28/starke-und-schwache-kunstliche-intelligenz/ (last access: 07-31-2018).

Wachtel, Andrew (2018): Universities in the Age of AI, online: https://www.project-syndicate.org/commentary/artificial-intelligence-higher-education-by-andrew-wachtel-2018-02?barrier=accesspaylog (last access: 07-31-2018).

Wagner, Kyle (2018): A Blended Environment: The Future of AI and Education, online: http://www.gettingsmart.com/2018/01/a-blended-environment-the-future-of-ai-and-education/ (last access: 07-31-2018).

Williams-Grut, Oscar (2017): Banks are looking to use artificial intelligence in almost every part of their business: Here's how it can boost profits, online: https://www.businessinsider.de/ai-in-financial-services-2017-11?r=UK&IR=T (last access: 07-31-2018).

Woyke, Elizabeth (2018): Economies can't ignore human needs if they want to benefit from automation, online: https://www.technologyreview.com/s/611348/economies-cant-ignore-human-needs-if-they-want-to-benefit-from-automation/ (last access: 07-31-2018).

Wray, Adam (2017): How To Prepare Your Company For The Internet Of Things, online: https://www.forbes.com/sites/forbestechcouncil/2017/02/14/how-to-prepare-your-company-for-the-internet-of-things/#3576d4d567e8 (last access: 07-31-2018).

Zeitfracht Medien GmbH
Ferdinand-Jühlke-Straße 7
99095 Erfurt, Deutschland
produktsicherheit@kolibri360.de